The Mourning After:

Healing Grief through Mediumship
&
Learning to Live and Love Again After Loss

Dr. Lakara E. Foster

Psychic Medium & Minister

Copyright © 2023 by Dr. Lakara E. Foster

All rights reserved. No part of this book may be reproduced in any form on by an electronic or mechanical means, including information storage and retrieval systems, without permission in writing from the publisher, except by a reviewer who may quote brief passages in a review.

Welcome to The Mourning After

Dear Reader,

I am honored to introduce you to a powerful book called *The Mourning After*. This book is a guide to using mediumship as a healing tool for love and life after loss.

Loss is an inevitable part of life, and grief can leave us feeling lost, alone, and overwhelmed. *The Mourning After* offers a fresh perspective on grief and loss, rooted in the belief that we are all connected and that love never truly dies.

Using my experiences as a medium and minister, this book will guide you through the mourning process and show you how I connect with your loved ones who have passed. Mediumship can be a powerful tool for healing!

In The Mourning After, you will learn skills that will help to:

- Navigate the complex emotions of grief and find a path toward healing and renewal,
- Cultivate a deeper understanding of life and death and learn how to embrace the cycles of change and transformation,
- Recognize the messages of love and comfort by learning signs and symbols that Spirit uses to get our attention,

- And so much more.

If you have found this book, know it is not by chance or coincidence. Either your soul or the soul of a loved one has guided you to help embrace your grief with grace and courage. You may have lost a loved one or know someone who has, and you feel compelled to share what you are learning or seek a deeper understanding of life and death. Regardless of the reason, you are about to read the right book at the right time. This book is a guide that will help you understand the power of mediumship as a tool for healing and the human spirit's resilience in the face of loss. I hope *The Mourning After* brings you comfort, healing, and renewed hope for the future.

With warm regards,
Dr. Lakara Foster
Psychic Medium and Minister

Tables of Contents

Chapter One: An Awakened Soul: The Medium and The Minister 1

Chapter Two: Grief: The Universal Language of Loss 7

Chapter Three: Ancestral Whispers: The History and Roots of Mediumship 25

Chapter Four: Inner Workings: The Art, Heart, and Mechanics of Mediumship 37

Chapter Five: Embracing The Invisible Thread: The Deep Bond Between Grief and Mediumship 53

Chapter Six: The Myth of Untimely Death: Sacred Contracts and Soul's Knowing 61

Chapter Seven: The Wisdom of Spirit: Lessons from Beyond the Veil 71

Chapter Eight: I Hope You Dance: Opening Your Heart Again to Love ..85

Chapter Nine: From Sorrow to Serenity: Reconstructing Life After Loss 93

Chapter Ten: In Their Own Words: Stories of Healing and Resilience...107

Acknowledgments 127

Chapter One

An Awakened Soul:

The Medium and The Minister

"Awake my soul. The glory of the Lord is upon me."
~ **Lailah Gifty Akita**

A Soul Awakens

I am Dr. Lakara Foster, and I am a Psychic Medium! My mediumship abilities enable me to connect people with their loved ones who have passed to bring them messages of healing, closure, and peace. I was born and raised in New Orleans, Louisiana, a city widely known for its fantastic cuisine and mysterious culture related to the Spirit world.

My soul began to awaken in the heart of New Orleans, where the mighty Mississippi River meets the warm embrace of the Bayous. As a child, I immersed myself in the city's rich culture, history, and spiritual tapestry. New Orleans, known for its vibrant celebrations and deep-rooted traditions, was fertile ground for my spiritual journey.

I began recognizing psychic and mediumship phenomena as a young child. Seeing apparitions and hearing voices was a common occurrence and, surprisingly, did not frighten me as I assumed that this was the experience of all people. One of my earliest memories of this gift of mediumship, which I did not realize was unusual then, was while attending the funeral of my great-aunt at three years old. I was very aware that the body of my Aunt Eva was in the casket, but I was also clear that her spirit was sitting among us in the funeral parlor. I remember thinking, "Oh, this is cool…You get to go to your funeral when you die," not realizing that no one else was experiencing the spiritual presence.

Another early memory is getting the daily newspaper, divvying it, and giving everyone their favorite section. My brother would get the sports section, my mom would read the cover stories, and I would grab the comics and the obituaries. As I read those obituaries, I could feel the departed people with me. While obits never tell you how people passed, I always knew how they transitioned and other things not listed in the newspaper. I never talked about these experiences because they did not feel foreign or warrant any intervention. I honestly thought this was what everyone experienced. It was not until young adulthood that I realized this was a rare gift, unique only to a small percentage of people.

As a curious and empathic child, I was drawn to the city's spiritual undercurrents, which swirled through the cobblestone streets, hidden courtyards, and ancient live oaks. In addition, my inquisitive nature led me to explore the melting pot of beliefs and practices that made New Orleans a spiritual crossroads for generations. I soaked in every nuance, from the Catholicism that permeated the city's architecture and rituals to the West African traditions brought over by enslaved people that evolved into powerful spiritual practices.

On school field trips, we wandered through the city's historical places, visiting its famous cemeteries, where the departed seemed to speak through the elaborate and weathered tombs. Among the mausoleums and above-ground vaults, I felt a profound connection to the stories and spirits that lingered. Each visit became a pilgrimage, a testament to my deepening awareness of the unseen world.

As my understanding of New Orleans' spiritual culture grew, so did my gifts. I began recognizing my innate ability to sense and communicate with the spirit world. However, in the first-year dorm of Florida Agricultural and Mechanical University, my journey took a pivotal turn amid the unyielding sorrow of a fellow student experiencing grief from losing her aunt. Giving an impromptu reading to my dorm mate and connecting her to her deceased aunt, I realized my purpose—to become a bridge between the living and the departed.

I aim to serve as a beacon of hope and comfort to individuals seeking guidance and connection to the other side. My upbringing in New Orleans instilled in me a deep appreciation for the interconnectedness of all things and the sacred beauty beneath the surface of everyday life. In those formative years, I learned to listen to the whispers of the spirit world and understood the importance of sharing those messages with others, and I look forward to sharing a special message with you through these pages.

Through my work, I honor the spirits I communicate with and the vibrant city that shaped my journey. In the soulful rhythm of my visits back home to New Orleans, I continue to dance to the timeless beat of life, death, and the mysteries between.

In addition to being a psychic medium, I am also a minister. Now, perhaps you paused and thought to yourself, "Is that possible? Can one be a minister and a medium?" I am here to tell you, "Absolutely!"

As an African-American psychic medium and minister, I have had to navigate the often-conflicting worlds of spirituality and Christianity. I knew I would have to find a way to reconcile (more for others than myself) my spiritual gift of mediumship with my calling as a pastor in a Christian church. It was a challenging journey, and I faced much backlash and resistance.

One person who played a significant role in helping me reconcile my gift with my ministerial calling was Dr. Daniel Black. He is a renowned award-winning author and professor of African American Studies at Clark Atlanta University in Atlanta, Georgia. He has dedicated his life to educating and empowering others to liberate themselves by any means necessary.

When I first told Dr. Black of the dichotomy of my spiritual gift and ministerial calling, I was working on my doctoral degree and trying to find the words to express my identity as a psychic medium and pastor. Unfortunately, some members of my church and the Christian community who saw my gift as incompatible with their faith had quietly ostracized me.

Dr. Black listened to my story with compassion and understanding. He encouraged me to embrace my gift and to see it as a valuable tool for helping others. He reminded me that Jesus was a healer and a spiritual leader who used his gifts to help others and that there was nothing inherently un-Christian about using my psychic mediumship abilities in ministry. From there, I was inspired to study more people of the Bible whose path aligned with my unique spiritual gift. I found their stories intriguing and relatable, and I realized that my gift was not an anomaly and that great people in the Bible shared similar gifts. For example, Joseph, the son of Jacob, predicted the future by analyzing dreams, and Jesus conversed with Moses and Elijah, who had already departed on the Mount of Transfiguration. Both stories demonstrate the use of psychic and mediumship gifts in the Bible.

I also relentlessly studied the roles of psychics in other periods throughout history and how they impacted religion, relationships with God, world views, and how people interacted with each other. I discovered that mediums have played a significant role in religion throughout history. In ancient cultures, priests and priestesses often functioned as mediums between the gods and people, relaying messages from the divine. In recent times, mediums have played a key role in Spiritualism. This religious movement began in the 19th century and was based on the belief that the departed can communicate with the living through mediums. By studying the role of mediums in different religions, I have gained a deeper understanding of other cultures' spiritual practices and beliefs.

With Dr. Black's guidance and support, I began to explore my gift more fully. I started offering psychic and medium readings full-time. I saw firsthand how transformative these experiences were for people, especially those mourning the loss of loved ones.

Of course, not everyone was supportive of my new direction. I continued to face hostile responses from those who saw my gift threatening their faith. But because I knew this gift was from God, I stayed true to myself and my calling, even in the face of opposition.

Today, I am proud to be a psychic medium and a pastor. I have found a way to reconcile my spiritual gifts with my ministerial calling, and I know that I am making a positive difference in those around me. I am forever grateful to Dr. Black and the countless others who showed me that it was possible to be both a spiritual leader and a psychic medium and gave me the courage and support I needed to embrace my true self. I am grateful to you, dear reader, for the healing journey on which you will continue with this book as your guide.

My divine assignment is to provide evidence to God's children of God's promise of eternal life and to demonstrate that God furnished some of us with the gift of mediumship to provide such proof. This proof helps the grieving heal with grace and courage to learn to live and love again after loss. Therefore, I cannot stray from this belief as my steps have been ordered, and God is leading the way. I have done my part by using my gifts to translate Spirit's message into this guide. Now, you can do your part by allowing your soul to awaken and embrace the extraordinary power of mediumship as a transformative tool for healing the profound pain of grief.

Chapter Two

Grief: The Universal Language of Loss

"Grief is the price we pay for love."
~ **Dr. Colin Murray Parkes**

Lakara's Story

When I was five, I saw a girl on the school playground jumping double-dutch and thought, "Wow, she is an angel." I saw a glow around her and knew we would be best friends...and we were. I was too shy to ask if I could play. (Plus, I did not know how to jump.) Finally, she noticed me, grabbed my hand, pushed me to the front of the line, and said, "You got this." Stacy Davis was my big sister (although she was only nine months older), my best friend, confidant, rock, and biggest cheerleader for ten years. She had the type of spirit everyone loved because she was pure light.

We often dressed alike and were constantly told we looked alike, so we told people we were sisters. We even begged our parents to buy us the same clothes so we could easily continue passing as siblings. We did everything together. We went everywhere together. There was barely a moment when we were not together. We attended the same elementary school until sixth grade, and then, because I had moved to another area of town, we went to different middle and high schools. The distance did nothing to separate us as we continued to spend every weekend together visiting malls, going to fairs, talking on the phone to boys, and doing all the silly and beautiful things teenage girls do.

Stacy and I were so profoundly bonded that it makes sense that she is connected to one of my most profound mediumship experiences. It was a cold Friday evening in December 1989, and one of the rare occasions Stacy and I would not spend the weekend together. She was scheduled to help with a school dance while I attended my uncle's annual Christmas Party. That night, around 8 p.m., I was violently ill for about 15 minutes. I grew unexplainably cold and began shaking and vomiting profusely. My mom wondered if she should take me to the emergency room, but as quickly as the illness came, it passed, and there was no real explanation for the occurrence. I would not find out until the next day that I was extremely ill at the same time, my best friend of 10 years was slipping away from the earthly realm and ascending into heaven. Stacy died in a car accident that cold December evening, creating a massive void in my life. I lost one of my very first friends and soul mates.

We never know how loss, grief, or traumatic experiences will shape our lives. Often, we do not realize how much the sorrow and guilt we carry influences our capacity to grow and love. I think of her every day because her unconditional love for me helped shape the woman I have become. There are moments when I am still that awkward adolescent who needs her childhood best friend to push her to the forefront, demand that she shine, and remind her that she, too, is light. Words will never entirely express how much I miss her. I miss those simple days of secrets, sleepovers, summer camps, bubble gum, boys, dressing like twins, and feeling like life would be that simple forever.

The Evolution of Grief

Before we go any further, it is essential to briefly introduce the pioneering work of Dr. Elizabeth Kubler-Ross, a prominent figure in the field of grief and loss. Dr. Kubler-Ross was a Swiss-American psychiatrist and author whose groundbreaking research on the stages of grief revolutionized our understanding of how individuals cope with the process of dying and bereavement. Her seminal book, "On Death and Dying," published in 1969, introduced the world to the now-famous "Kubler-Ross Model" of the five stages of grief: denial, anger, bargaining, depression, and acceptance. Because other models have been formulated throughout the years, I have included additional stages that demonstrate the advancement in the study of grief.

The evolution of grief is a deeply personal and often non-linear process that individuals go through after experiencing a significant loss. It encompasses a range of emotional, psychological, and physical responses that change over time. While everyone's grief journey is unique, there are common stages and phases that many people may encounter. Understanding the evolution of grief can help individuals navigate this challenging experience with greater awareness and compassion.

1. Shock and Denial: The initial response to loss is often shock and disbelief. It can be challenging to accept the reality of the situation, leading to a temporary state of denial. This phase is a protective mechanism that allows individuals to gradually absorb the shock. It is a

natural reaction to the emotional impact of the loss and serves as a protective mechanism to help individuals cope with the overwhelming initial wave of emotions.

During this phase, individuals may exhibit numbness, disbelief, or a sense that the loss is unreal. They may also experience physical symptoms like fatigue, dizziness, or feeling "out of it." It is vital for individuals and their support systems to recognize that this phase is a normal response to an extraordinary event. This is a transitional phase that, in time, gives way to other stages of grief as individuals begin to process their feelings and move toward healing.

In understanding the "Shock and Denial" phase, individuals can acknowledge its significance in their grief journey and seek support when they feel ready to confront and work through their emotions in subsequent stages of grief.

2. Anger: This phase typically follows the initial shock and denial as individuals grapple with the reality of their loss. Anger is a natural emotional response during this time and is an integral part of the grieving process.

During the "Anger" phase, individuals may experience intense emotions, including frustration, resentment, and a sense of injustice. These emotions can be directed at various targets, including themselves, the person they have lost, external circumstances, and even a higher power. It is crucial to understand that anger during grief is normal and healthy.

Anger often arises because individuals are trying to make sense of their loss, and they may feel a sense of powerlessness or unfairness in the situation. It is an emotional expression of the pain and sadness they are experiencing. Acknowledging and processing this anger is an essential part of the healing journey.

Support from friends, family, or a mental health professional can be invaluable during the "Anger" phase. It is essential to allow oneself to feel and express these emotions safely and constructively, as doing so can contribute to the overall healing process and eventually lead to a greater sense of acceptance and understanding.

3. Bargaining: During the "Bargaining" phase, individuals may engage in various behaviors and thought processes, including making promises or dealing with a higher power to regain control or reverse the loss. This can involve seeking alternative solutions or imagining scenarios where the loss could be undone.

The act of bargaining reflects the profound desire to alleviate the pain and suffering associated with grief. It attempts to find meaning or purpose in the face of the loss as individuals struggle to make sense of their changed reality.

It is essential to recognize that bargaining is a normal human response to grief. It allows individuals to express their emotions and process their grief, even if the bargaining may not change the outcome. Over time, individuals often gradually shift towards acceptance and a deeper understanding of their loss as they move through the grieving process.

4. Depression: This stage is a natural and significant part of the grieving process, and it often follows the initial shock, denial, anger, and bargaining phases.

During the "Depression" phase, individuals grapple with profound sadness and emotional pain as they come to terms with the reality of their loss. It is common for people in this phase to experience feelings of hopelessness, loneliness, and despair. Grief can feel overwhelming during this stage, and it may seem like the pain will never subside.

It is crucial to emphasize the importance of seeking support during the "Depression" phase. This support can come from friends, family, support groups, or mental health professionals who can guide and assist in navigating the depths of grief. Sharing one's feelings and experiences with a supportive network can be vital to healing.

It is also worth noting that experiencing depression during grief is a normal response to an extraordinary event. It is not a sign of weakness but rather a reflection of the profound emotional impact that loss can have on an individual's life. With time and support, individuals often find that, while the pain of grief may never completely disappear, it becomes more manageable, and moments of light and healing can emerge.

5. Acceptance: "Acceptance" is a pivotal point in the grieving process, representing a significant shift in how individuals relate to their loss.

In this phase, individuals come to terms with the reality of their loss. It is important to emphasize that acceptance does not imply forgetting or moving on from the loss. Instead, it signifies the beginning of integration. It is a point at which individuals adapt to life without the person they have lost.

Acceptance allows individuals to live with their grief more comfortably. It does not eliminate grief, but it changes the relationship with it. Grief becomes a part of their life story, and individuals find ways to coexist with it. They may still experience moments of sadness, longing, or remembrance, but these emotions are no longer as all-consuming as in earlier stages of grief.

During the "Acceptance" phase, individuals often experience a gradual shift toward more emotional stability and resilience. They may find the capacity to engage more fully in their daily lives while carrying the memory of their loss.

It is important to remember that the grieving process is highly individual, and not everyone experiences each phase in the same way or order. Some individuals may move through these phases more quickly or revisit certain stages multiple times. Regardless of the path taken, "Acceptance" represents an essential milestone on the journey toward healing and finding a new equilibrium in life after loss.

6. Finding Meaning: During this phase, individuals go beyond simply accepting the reality of their loss; they actively seek ways to find purpose and significance in their grief journey. This can take various forms, such as:

- Personal Growth: Some individuals use their grief to catalyze personal growth and self-discovery. They may embark on a journey of self-improvement, exploring new interests or hobbies, and developing a deeper understanding of themselves.

- Connection: Grief can create a powerful sense of empathy and compassion. Many people in this phase seek connection with others who have experienced loss. Sharing their stories and offering support can be profoundly healing.

- Honoring Memories: Finding meaning often involves honoring the memory of the person or thing they have lost. This can include creating memorials or altars, participating in charitable activities, or carrying on traditions that pay tribute to their loved ones.

- Advocacy and Awareness: Some individuals channel their grief into advocacy work or raising awareness about the causes related to their loss. This can be a way to ensure that their loved one's legacy lives on and contributes to positive change.

- Spiritual Exploration: Grief can lead individuals to explore their spiritual beliefs and find solace and meaning in their faith or spiritual practices.

Finding meaning in grief is a transformative aspect of the grief journey, as it allows individuals to transcend the pain and suffering associated with loss and discover a sense of purpose and fulfillment. It is important to acknowledge that this phase does not erase grief but helps individuals integrate it into their lives to foster growth and healing.

7. Rebuilding and Healing: The "Rebuilding and Healing" phase within grief's evolution is precise and uplifting. This phase signifies a pivotal turning point in the grieving process, symbolizing a transition from the acute pain of loss to a more manageable and adaptable state of being.

During the "Rebuilding and Healing" phase, individuals rebuild their lives while carrying the cherished memory of their loss. It is crucial to underscore that this phase does not entail forgetting or fully recovering from the loss. Instead, it symbolizes progress and personal growth, where individuals learn to integrate their grief into the fabric of their lives.

Key attributes characterizing the "Rebuilding and Healing" phase encompass a renewed engagement with life's daily rhythms, including work and social activities. Amid this, individuals may rediscover a semblance of normalcy while maintaining a deep acknowledgment and reverence for their grief.

In this phase, the intensity of pain, although never entirely vanishing, often subsides, providing individuals with more frequent moments of emotional equilibrium and, at times, even glimpses of joy. Rather than causing overwhelming distress, the memories of the person become wellsprings of comfort and connection. Special occasions and milestones are commemorated in ways that honor the enduring legacy of their loved ones.

Moreover, self-care and well-being are heightened as individuals recognize the importance of tending to their physical and emotional health while navigating life with the ever-present companion of grief. Through this journey, individuals in the "Rebuilding and Healing" phase embody remarkable strength. They carry forward the invaluable lessons and experiences from their grief journey, frequently becoming a source of inspiration and support for others enduring their grief.

The "Rebuilding and Healing" phase is a testament to the extraordinary human capacity for adaptation and growth in the face of loss. It shines a spotlight on the indomitable resilience inherent in individuals who have navigated the turbulent waters of grief and emerged on the other side, not unscathed by their experiences but imbued with newfound strength and wisdom, ready to face life's challenges with a renewed sense of purpose and resilience.

8. Continuing Bonds: The "Continuing Bonds" phase in grief's evolution is compassionate and insightful. This phase represents a profound shift in how individuals relate to the person they have lost, emphasizing the ongoing connection and significance of that relationship even after death.

During the "Continuing Bonds" phase, individuals seek healthy and constructive ways to maintain a connection with the person they have lost. This includes honoring memories through creating memorials, dedicating special events, or preserving keepsakes. Additionally, this phase often involves deepening spiritual or metaphysical beliefs as individuals explore the idea of a continued bond with their loved ones beyond the physical realm. Some may even feel a sense of guidance or presence from their loved ones, turning to this connection for support and inspiration.

Many people in this phase are inspired to live in a way that reflects the values, qualities, or passions of the person they have lost, actively working to carry forward their loved one's legacy. Sharing stories and memories of their loved ones with friends and family becomes a meaningful way to keep the memory alive and celebrate the impact that person had on their lives. The "Continuing Bonds" phase is a healthy and constructive aspect of the grief journey. It offers comfort, inspiration, and a sense of ongoing connection, all of which contribute to the healing process, allowing individuals to carry their loved one's memories throughout their lives.

9. Integration: This phase represents a profound transformation in how individuals incorporate grief into their lives, allowing them to find joy and happiness without guilt.

As individuals progress through the "Integration" phase, grief becomes seamlessly woven into the fabric of their life story. It ceases to be a separate, all-consuming entity and becomes an integral part of who they are. This integration is a testament to their capacity to adapt.

In this phase, individuals learn to live with their grief while moving forward with their lives. It does not entail forgetting or erasing the memory of their loss but instead finding a way to coexist with it that does not impede their ability to experience joy and happiness.

One of the remarkable aspects of the "Integration" phase is that it liberates individuals from the burden of guilt that may have accompanied their moments of happiness during earlier stages of grief. They understand that finding moments of light and laughter is not disloyal or disrespectful to their loved ones. Instead, it is a testament to their ability to honor the memory of their loved ones while continuing to embrace the full spectrum of human emotions.

Ultimately, the "Integration" phase signifies a profound healing and transformation. It allows individuals to carry their grief as part of their life's narrative while moving forward with a sense of wholeness, joy, and acceptance. This integration is evidence of the human spirit's remarkable fortitude and capacity for growth and healing in the face of loss.

It is important to note that not everyone experiences every stage of grief, and the order and duration of each phase can vary widely. Grief is a unique and individual process, and there is no right or wrong way to grieve. Seeking support from friends, family, or a mental health professional can be invaluable in navigating the evolution of grief and finding a path toward healing.

The Powerful Force of Grief

Grief is an inevitable part of the human experience. No matter who we are or where we come from, we will eventually encounter loss. This shared understanding of loss connects us fundamentally and creates a sense of unity and empathy.

We all know that grief is a complex, powerful, and transformative force that can touch us in the depths of our hearts, affecting every aspect of our lives. It has a multifaceted impact on our emotions, relationships, and sense of self. Understanding the many faces of grief allows us to embrace the healing journey with greater self-awareness and compassion. Through this process, we can discover the power to heal, grow, and find renewed hope and purpose in the face of loss.

Despite the unique ways we experience and express grief, common threads unite us all. The emotions we feel – sadness, anger, guilt, relief – are shared experiences that transcend personal and cultural boundaries. Recognizing these commonalities can foster empathy, understanding, and connection with grieving others. While grief is a universal experience, how we express and cope with it can vary across cultures and traditions. Rituals, mourning practices, and beliefs about the afterlife differ worldwide. Yet, they share a common goal: to honor the deceased's memory and comfort the living.

Sorrow can bring forth a whirlwind of emotions, leaving us feeling like we are on an ever-changing rollercoaster. It is important to remember that there is no "right" way to grieve and that these emotions are all part of the natural healing process. By acknowledging and honoring our feelings, we can allow ourselves the space to navigate our grief with self-compassion and grace.

The loss of a loved one can also have a profound impact on our relationships with others. We may find that some relationships grow stronger as we lean on one another for support and comfort. Other relationships may be tested as we struggle to find a new balance in the absence of our loved ones. It is essential to recognize how grief affects our relationships and seek open and honest communication with those around us as we navigate this challenging time.

It is crucial to remember that healing is a journey, not a destination. By honoring our emotions, nurturing our relationships, and cultivating self-care, we can embrace the healing process with openness and self-compassion. As we learn to integrate our grief into our lives, we can discover the strength and resilience within each of us.

I have discovered that we do not heal from grief; we heal through grief, and as we move through the grieving process, we may find that our sense of self is altered. We may question our identity, beliefs, and values to find meaning in our loss. This self-discovery process can be challenging and transformative, encouraging us to grow and evolve in response to our pain. By embracing this journey of self-exploration, we can learn to integrate our grief into our lives and emerge as a more authentic version of ourselves.

Acknowledging and Validating the Unique Experience of Grief

Grief, as an inherent part of our human experience, can manifest in countless ways, often leaving us feeling lonely, overwhelmed, and unsure of how to heal. It is essential as a medium to share my wisdom on acknowledging and validating the unique experience of grief. In addition, I aim to offer comfort, understanding, and guidance as you navigate the complexities of your healing journey.

Grief is as unique and individual as the person experiencing it. We each have ways of processing and expressing the pain of loss, and it is vital to honor these differences. Some may find solace in solitude, while others seek comfort in the company of loved ones. Some may turn to their faith or spirituality, while others explore creative outlets for their emotions. There is no right or wrong way to grieve, and we must learn to respect and honor our unique journey and those of others. I tell clients often, "Do not let others dictate your grieving process!" They find this statement enlightening, empowering, and relieving from the expectations around grieving that others try to place upon them.

One of the most profound ways to validate the unique experience of grief is through acknowledgment. We create space for healing and growth by openly acknowledging the pain and heartache accompanying loss. By recognizing the validity of our emotions and allowing ourselves to feel them thoroughly, we can begin to process our grief and find a path forward.

Acknowledge the pain, the sadness, the anger, and the fear. Permit yourself to feel these emotions without judgment or guilt. Remember, your feelings are a natural and necessary part of the grieving process, and they deserve to be honored and respected.

We can also extend the gift of acknowledgment to others by validating their grief experiences and offering empathy, understanding, and support. When we validate the grief of others, we communicate that their feelings are heard and valued, providing a powerful source of comfort and connection during a time of significant vulnerability and pain. Remember that you are not alone in your turmoil; we are all united in our experience of loss and our pursuit of healing. May we walk together on this journey, supporting one another with love, compassion, and grace.

Chapter 2: Grief: The Universal Language of Loss

Lesson: Exploring the Dimensions of Grief

In this lesson, we will delve into the multifaceted nature of grief, understanding that it is a universal language spoken in response to loss. Grief takes various forms, and recognizing its dimensions can aid healing.

- **Dimensions of Grief**: Grief can manifest emotionally, physically, mentally, and spiritually. Explore these dimensions to gain a comprehensive understanding of your own grief experience.

Exercise: Identifying Your Unique Grief Triggers

1. List situations, places, or objects that trigger your grief. These triggers may include anniversaries, certain songs, or even specific scents.

2. Next to each trigger, write down the emotions or physical sensations it evokes. Be as specific as possible. For example, a particular song may make you feel sadness or bring tears to your eyes.

3. Reflect on why these triggers affect you the way they do. Is there a specific memory or connection associated with each trigger? Understanding the underlying reasons can provide insight into your grief.

Activity: Write a Letter to Your Grief

1. Set aside time to write a heartfelt letter to your grief. Address it as if it were a person or a presence in your life.

2. In your letter, express your feelings openly. Share your anger, sadness, confusion, and any other emotions you have experienced. Be honest and raw in your writing.

3. Write about how grief has affected your life, relationships, and daily experiences. Reflect on the challenges it has posed and the lessons it may have brought.

4. Close the letter with a message of acknowledgment and acceptance. It could be something like, "I understand that you are a part of my journey, and I am willing to work through this pain and find healing."

This lesson encourages you to explore the dimensions of grief and identify your unique grief triggers. You can begin the journey toward healing and understanding by acknowledging and addressing your grief. Writing a letter to your grief can be a powerful step in this process, allowing you to express and release your emotions.

Chapter Three
Ancestral Whispers:
The History and Roots of Mediumship

"In the quiet moments of our lives, we can hear the eternal whispers of those we've lost, gently guiding us with their wisdom and love, even from beyond the veil."

~ **Unknown**

Mother Catherine's Story

Mother Catherine Seals remains a mysterious figure, with limited information and only a few photographs to document her life. Much of what we know about her is based on hearsay and oral tradition. She was known for her extraordinary healing abilities, unique character, musical talents, and walking barefoot in the neighborhood. These things left an indelible impression on those who encountered her.

Mother Catherine's journey began as Catherine Nanny Cowans, a young girl from Kentucky. She faced hardships and abusive relationships, leading her to seek help from a spiritual healer named Brother Isaiah. Unfortunately, he turned her away due to her African-American heritage, leaving her feeling rejected and hopeless. In a moment of prayer, she received a spiritual visitation that guided her to create her organization to help and heal those in need.

Under the guidance of Mother Leafy Anderson, the founder of the spiritual church movement in New Orleans, Catherine trained to become a spiritual mother herself. She embraced her calling and established her independent church, the Temple of the Innocent Blood, in the Lower 9th Ward in 1922. The church became a sanctuary for people of all races, defying social norms and flattening racial hierarchies. Mother Catherine's healing powers and rituals drew people from all levels of society, transcending barriers and offering hope to those in need.

Mother Catherine's temple, accompanied by a manger, was a sacred space for spiritual ceremonies and gatherings. The atmosphere was enchanting, with hundreds of lamps illuminating the surroundings. Her clay sculptures adorned the room, and despite the muddy terrain surrounding the compound, people ventured through knee-deep mud to seek her healing.

The name "Temple of the Innocent Blood" symbolized Mother Catherine's dedication to helping marginalized women, particularly those who were abandoned and abused. Her temple became a place of refuge and empowerment, challenging societal norms and offering solace to those who sought her guidance.

The temple's popularity and Mother Catherine's healing reputation led to occasional arson attacks, reflecting the resistance and fear her spiritual practices evoked in some individuals. However, her impact on the lives of countless people continued to grow, transcending racial boundaries and inspiring awe in those who witnessed her ceremonies.

Mother Catherine's influence extended beyond her lifetime, as her legacy lived on through the spiritual churches that honored her as their patron saint.

While the spiritual churches in the Lower 9th Ward eventually declined, and Hurricane Katrina further dispersed the remaining spiritual communities, Mother Catherine's memory and impact endure. Her story, like that of legendary figures such as Daniel Boone or Davy Crockett, persists through the oral tradition and the collective memory of the people. Mother Catherine Seals, the spiritual pioneer of New Orleans, remains a symbol of resilience, healing, and the power of spiritual connection in the face of adversity.

The Roots of Mediumship

Mediumship is not a new phenomenon. Its roots run deep, intertwining with the threads of human history and transcending cultural boundaries. Since ancient times, across various civilizations and cultures, there has been a profound belief in the existence of an unseen realm and the ability to communicate with spirits or departed souls. From ancient Greece's revered oracles to Indigenous peoples' spiritual practices, mediumship has served as a bridge between the earthly and the ethereal, offering guidance, healing, and a connection to the divine. In this chapter, we embark on a journey to explore those roots, delving into the rich array of traditions, beliefs, and practices that have shaped this timeless phenomenon. Through this exploration, we seek to deepen our understanding of the universal human longing for connection beyond the physical realm and the enduring role of mediums as conduits between worlds.

Mediumship in the Ancient World

The concept of mediumship dates back thousands of years, with evidence of spirit communication found in ancient civilizations such as Egypt, Mesopotamia, and China. In these cultures, priests and shamans often served as intermediaries between the living and the spirit world, performing rituals and divination to seek guidance and wisdom from the beyond.

In the ancient world, mediumship was a revered and respected practice. Mediums were believed to be able to communicate with the spirit world and connect with loved ones who had passed on. These individuals were often sought out for their wisdom and insight and revered for their ability to bridge the gap between the physical and spiritual realms.

In many cultures, mediumship was a sacred gift the gods or ancestors bestowed upon specific individuals. Consequently, mediums were often held in high esteem and considered prominent members of their communities. They were called upon to provide guidance and support and were believed to have a direct line to the divine.

The Greek and Roman Roots of Mediumship

Mediumship has its roots deeply intertwined with ancient Greek and Roman cultures. In both civilizations, the belief in an afterlife was prevalent, and connecting with departed souls was significant. The Greeks, for instance, conducted rituals and seances to summon spirits, seeking guidance from ancestors or the departed. The Oracle of Delphi, a famous institution in ancient Greece, was renowned for its prophetic abilities and communication with the divine, where the priestess Pythia would enter a trance-like state and deliver cryptic messages from the god Apollo.

In Roman society, mediums, often called "ventriloquists," were consulted to communicate with spirits for advice or to predict the future. These practices were spiritual and integral to political and personal decision-making. These and other ancient cultures laid the foundation for the diverse and evolving field of spiritual communication we encounter today, highlighting the enduring human fascination with the mysteries of the spirit world.

The Influence of Eastern Traditions

Eastern traditions, such as Hinduism, Buddhism, and Daoism, have also contributed significantly to the development of mediumship. The belief in reincarnation and the soul's continued existence after death is central to many Eastern philosophies, with mediums often guiding the transition from one life to the next. In these traditions, mediumship is usually practiced in the context of spiritual development and the pursuit of enlightenment.

The African Roots of Mediumship

The African roots of mediumship hold a sacred space in the cultural and spiritual tapestry of many African and African diaspora communities. We must understand that these roots run deep and are the essence of our connection with the divine. African spiritual traditions, such as those practiced by the Yoruba, Igbo, and Akan peoples, emphasize the importance of maintaining a connection with the ancestors, with mediums often serving as healers and spiritual advisors within their communities.

In the heart of Africa, mediumship has been a cornerstone of spiritual practice for generations. From the wise griots who shared our ancestors' stories to the revered shamans and healers who communed with the spirit world, our people have known the power of this sacred connection. It has been a guiding light in our darkest hours, nurturing our souls and illuminating our paths through life's trials and triumphs.

African Americans carry a rich and enduring connection to mediumship, passed down from our African ancestors. Enslaved Africans arrived in America under dire conditions, often stripped of their cultural and spiritual traditions, forbidden from practicing their ancestral religions, and subjected to the oppressive forces of slavery. The African diaspora began to take shape in this oppressive environment as people from different African regions were forced together.

Despite these harrowing circumstances, African people believed the spirit world was integral to their existence. They believed in the presence of ancestral spirits and the importance of maintaining a connection with them. This belief has not been extinguished, and it has become the ember of hope and resilience that continues to burn in the hearts of African Americans.

As the tradition of communicating with spirits persisted in the face of adversity, it underwent a process of adaptation and fusion. Enslaved Africans began incorporating elements from various African cultures and elements from Native American, European, and Christian traditions, such as ancestor veneration, herbal medicine, divination, and music. This amalgamation of beliefs and practices eventually gave rise to a unique and syncretic form of spirituality that we now recognize as African-American spirituality. It blended the Christian faith imposed upon the enslaved population with African spiritual practices, resulting in distinctive forms of worship, such as the "ring shout," and the development of African-American denominations like the African Methodist Episcopal Church (AME) and the Baptist Church.

This evolving spirituality was not only a means of coping with the immense hardships of slavery but also a source of empowerment. It provided a sense of identity, community, and hope in the face of brutality and oppression. It became a powerful tool for resilience and resistance, fostering a deep understanding of cultural continuity and pride among African Americans who had the remarkable ability to adapt, preserve, and transform their cultural and spiritual heritage in the face of unimaginable challenges.

Mediums and spiritual leaders played a crucial role in this evolving spiritual landscape. They served as bridges between the African ancestral heritage and the new cultural context in which they found themselves. These gifted individuals continued to communicate with the spirit world, providing guidance, healing, and comfort to their communities.

Mediumship continues to be an essential part of daily life in many African-American communities. Families gather for various rituals, including prayer and song, to connect with their ancestors and seek guidance. These practices strengthen familial bonds and foster community, providing solace and healing during loss.

The significance of these rituals and celebrations cannot be overstated. They connect us to something greater than ourselves and remind us that we are part of a larger spiritual community. Whether rooted in traditional African spirituality or modern-day church services, they allow us to honor our ancestors and connect with the divine. They serve as a reminder of the continuousness of life and the presence of our loved ones beyond the physical world.

By embracing our ancestral inheritance, we derive strength from the knowledge and counsel transmitted across generations, enabling us to persevere through the challenges and hardships of bereavement. The practice of mediumship holds a deep and meaningful place in African culture, and its fusion with our spiritual journey is a testament to our cultural heritage. Our history is steeped in Spirit.

The Spiritualist Movement: A Modern Revival

The Spiritualist movement, which gained popularity in the mid-19th century, marked a significant turning point in the history of mediumship. Rooted in the belief in the soul's survival after death, Spiritualism gave rise to the modern practice of mediumship as we know it today. The movement emerged in a time of great social and scientific upheaval when people sought comfort and reassurance in the face of rapid industrialization, social inequality, and the growing influence of scientific rationalism.

During this transformative period, the Fox Sisters, Margaret, Kate, and Leah, were prominent figures in the Spiritualist movement. In 1848, in the small town of Hydesville, New York, the sisters claimed to communicate with spirits through mysterious rapping. Their demonstrations of spirit communication captivated audiences and sparked a surge of interest in spirit contact that would sweep across America and Europe. As news of their abilities spread, they became celebrities, drawing large crowds to witness their mediumistic sessions.

The Fox Sisters played a pivotal role in popularizing Spiritualism and establishing it as a legitimate spiritual practice. Their experiences validated the belief in an afterlife and allowed countless individuals to explore their mediumistic abilities. One notable outcome of the Spiritualist movement was the establishment of Lily Dale, a small town in western New York, which became a hub for Spiritualists and mediums worldwide. Founded in 1879, Lily Dale serves as a sanctuary for spiritual seekers and a center for the practice and study of mediumship. It stands as a living testament to the enduring legacy of the Spiritualist movement and its profound impact on the development and recognition of mediumship as a legitimate spiritual practice.

Numerous renowned mediums and spiritual leaders have graced Lily Dale's Historic Lakeside Auditorium stage since its 1879 inception. It has borne witness to the enigmatic séances of Abraham Lincoln, where the great leader sought solace and guidance during tumultuous times, and the pioneering spirit of Susan B. Anthony, a champion of women's rights, who found a voice even beyond the earthly realm, sharing her vision for equality and justice with eager audiences. In recent years, audiences have also witnessed the profound insights and teachings of psychic mediums John Edward, Lisa Williams, and spiritual guru Deepak Chopra. And, in a significant milestone, in August 2023, I had the honor and privilege to emerge as the first African-American medium to step onto this sacred stage, breaking barriers and expanding the tapestry of spiritual inclusivity at Lily Dale. My presence symbolizes the evolution of this extraordinary spiritual community and the power of diversity and representation in the realm of mediumship. Together, these luminous figures illuminate the diverse and inclusive tapestry of Lily Dale, where history, spirituality, and progress converge in remarkable ways.

Mediumship Today: A Diverse Landscape

Despite the passage of time, the practice of mediumship endures and continues to be a source of comfort and healing for many people today. While the methods and techniques may have changed, the fundamental belief that our loved ones continue to exist in some form beyond this life remains a powerful and comforting notion. Whether we seek guidance from mediums, turn to religion or spirituality, or find our unique way of connecting with the divine, the practice of mediumship reminds us that we are never truly alone and that our loved ones continue to be with us in spirit. The history and roots of mediumship paint a rich and diverse picture of humanity's ongoing quest for connection with the spirit world.

Chapter 3: Ancestral Whispers: The History and Roots of Mediumship

Lesson: Delving into the History of Mediumship

In this lesson, we will embark on a journey into the rich history of mediumship. Understanding the roots and evolution of this practice will deepen your connection to it.

- **History of Mediumship**: Explore the historical origins of mediumship, including its presence in various cultures and traditions.

Exercise: Researching Your Ancestral Roots

1. Begin by researching your family history. Try to trace your lineage as far back as possible. Online genealogy websites and family records can be valuable resources.

2. Identify any ancestors or relatives who may have had a connection to spiritual practices, mediumship, or intuitive abilities. Look for stories, traditions, or cultural practices that hint at such connections.

3. If you discover any ancestral links to mediumship or spiritual practices, write down what you have found and consider how this ancestral knowledge may resonate with your path.

Activity: Ancestor Altar Creation

1. Find a quiet and sacred space in your home to create an ancestor altar. This could be a shelf, table, or any area where you feel strongly connected to your ancestors.

2. Gather items representing your ancestors and their cultural or spiritual heritage. These items can include photographs, heirlooms, candles, incense, flowers, or symbolic objects.

3. Arrange these items on your ancestor altar with intention and reverence. Light a candle and take a moment to connect with your ancestors. You may wish to pray or express gratitude for their presence.

4. Spend time at your ancestor altar regularly, whether to meditate, offer prayers, or sit in quiet reflection. This practice can help you feel more connected to your ancestral roots and the history of mediumship.

This lesson encourages you to delve into the history of mediumship and explore your ancestral roots. By creating an ancestor altar, you can establish a tangible connection with your ancestors and the spiritual practices that may have influenced your family's heritage. Understanding the history of mediumship in your lineage can deepen your appreciation for this ancient practice.

Chapter Four
Inner Workings:
The Art, Heart, and Mechanics of Mediumship

"The bonds of love connect us to the other side."
~ **John Edward**

I am often asked how I can communicate with the departed. How can I know how they died, what kind of car they drove, their favorite food, how many children they had, and even their birth and death date? I try to explain to people what Spirit has taught me over the years and how this gift of mediumship works.

Mediumship is a fascinating and intricate practice that involves communicating with the spirit world. Mediums, those who possess this gift, can connect the physical and spiritual planes and deliver messages from loved ones who have passed away. During their heightened awareness, mediums use their abilities, such as clairvoyance (seeing images), clairaudience (hearing voices or sounds), and clairsentience (experiencing physical sensations or emotions), to receive and transmit information from spirits. This can include seeing images, hearing voices, or sensing emotions. Mediumship is a valuable source of comfort and insight for those seeking answers or connecting with their departed loved ones. It is a powerful tool for grieving individuals, as it can provide a sense of peace and closure. Mediumship can also be viewed as a spiritual practice that suggests that life continues beyond this physical realm. By connecting with the spiritual world, people can find a deeper understanding of their place in the universe and discover meaning and purpose.

There are two distinct types of mediums: physical mediums and mental mediums. Physical mediumship is where the medium is believed to produce physical phenomena that others can witness. These phenomena can range from the movement of objects to the appearance of apparitions or materialized objects. Physical mediumship is often considered the most challenging and controversial form of mediumship, as it is difficult to produce and replicate under controlled conditions. However, for believers, physical mediumship provides a tangible connection to the afterlife and offers proof of the existence of spirits beyond the physical realm.

Mental mediumship is a specific form of mediumship in which the medium perceives and interprets messages from the spirit world using their psychic faculties rather than through physical manifestations. The process often involves the medium attuning themselves to the subtle vibrations of the spiritual realm, enabling them to access and interpret information from those who have passed on. This can be achieved through various means, including clairvoyance, clairaudience, and clairsentience. The medium serves as a conduit, translating these impressions into messages that can be shared with the living. I am a mental medium.

As a medium, my process involves connecting with the spirit realm to communicate with loved ones who have passed on, offering comfort and closure to those seeking it. I approach each session with compassion and respect, striving to create a safe and nurturing environment for my clients. I give each client my spiel regarding my process, what they can expect during a reading, and the limitations of our interaction. I tell them:

"I do not talk to the dead; there is no such thing as dead. We are energy, and energy cannot be created or destroyed. We are pure energy before we enter these bodies, while in them, and when we depart from them, leaving behind this physical shell. I have no control over who comes through, but if it is someone you are hoping to come through or have been thinking about, that is usually who comes through. Spirit communicates with me through signs and symbols, and I will share with you what those signs and symbols have come to mean to me over the years, and we will make sense of the messages we hear."

"I don't talk to the dead."

I am sure this first statement catches people off guard because people believe that mediums speak with dead people. However, it can bring comfort and peace when we understand that we do not die but rather transition to a different realm. We can begin to see death as a natural part of the cycle of life, and we can find contentment in the knowledge that our loved ones are still with us in some way. Mediumship can help to facilitate this understanding by providing evidence of the continuity of life.

Many spiritual traditions believe in an afterlife or a different realm beyond the physical world. One of the critical concepts in spirituality is the understanding that we do not die but instead transition to a different realm. Many spiritual traditions believe in reincarnation, where the soul continues a journey of growth and evolution beyond physical departure.

Others believe in an afterlife, where the soul exists in a different realm beyond the physical world.

"All we are is energy."

Our souls are much more than just physical bodies. They are an eternal and indestructible energy that exists beyond the physical realm. This energy is the essence of who we are and connects us to the universe and all living things. Our souls are the source of our consciousness, creativity, and deepest emotions. They are the essence of our being, the spark that ignites our passions, and the driving force behind our actions. This energy is what gives us our unique personalities, our individuality, and our sense of purpose. It is what makes us feel alive and gives meaning to our lives. Our souls are not limited to one physical body but can inhabit various forms throughout the universe. They are infinite and boundless and continue to exist even after our physical bodies perish.

When we recognize and connect with this energy within ourselves, we tap into a profound sense of inner peace and harmony. We become more aware of our true selves, deepest desires, and connections to the universe. We become more attuned to the needs of others, and we develop a greater sense of empathy and compassion. This energy is what makes us human, and it is what connects us to the world around us.

While our souls are energy, it is still so much more than that. They are the essence of our being, the source of our consciousness, and the driving force behind our actions. When we recognize and connect with this energy within ourselves, we tap into a profound sense of inner peace and harmony. We become more aware of our true selves and connection to the universe and develop greater empathy and compassion for all living things.

"We are energy before we enter these bodies."

The idea that energy exists before our souls inhabit our bodies is a concept in many philosophical and spiritual traditions. It suggests that our souls are not separate entities that come into being when we are born but rather eternal and indestructible energies that have always existed and will continue to exist long after our physical bodies have passed on. This energy is often called life force or vital energy and is considered the foundation of our physical and spiritual existence.

In some Eastern spiritual practices, this energy is known as "prana" or "chi," it is believed to flow through our bodies, impacting our physical, mental, and emotional well-being. Our thoughts, emotions, and actions can influence this life force, and our lifestyle and environment can balance or disrupt it. It is important to recognize the significance of this energy and take steps to maintain its balance and harmony in our lives.

It is fascinating how some spiritual beliefs suggest that our souls can inhabit various forms throughout the universe and are not limited to just one physical body. Again, this concept of reincarnation acknowledges that we are more than just our current experiences in this lifetime. In the African-American community, we often recognize this more profound wisdom in people by saying things like "That's an old soul" or "That child has been here before." It is a way of respecting those who have come before us and acknowledging the spiritual connections that bind us all. By acknowledging infinite wisdom within each of us, we can cultivate a healthy and balanced life force that can lead to optimal physical, mental, and spiritual health. This belief in the interconnectedness of all things reminds us that there is more to our existence than just our physical bodies.

"We are energy while we are in these bodies."

The concept of the soul as an energetic entity has fascinated humans for centuries. While it is impossible to prove the existence of the soul scientifically, many spiritual and religious traditions suggest that the soul is a non-physical entity beyond the confines of our physical bodies.

One way to understand the soul as energy is to think of it as a vibrational frequency that permeates every aspect of our being. Our thoughts, emotions, and actions all generate power, and this energy creates a resonance that is unique to everyone. This resonance is often called the soul or the spirit and is thought to be our essence.

While it is difficult to fully comprehend the nature of the soul and its existence as energy, this concept holds powerful and transformative potential for our lives. It provides a sense of purpose and meaning as we recognize that our actions and intentions profoundly impact the energy we generate and the legacy we leave behind.

"We will be energy once we depart from these bodies."

Many spiritual and philosophical traditions suggest that when we depart from our physical bodies, our souls continue to exist as energy. One way to understand this concept is to think of the soul as living beyond the limitations of time and space. This means that the soul is not bound by the laws of physics that govern our physical bodies, and it is free to travel and exist in other dimensions and realms.

According to many spiritual and religious traditions, the soul may continue its journey after physical death through various means, such as reincarnation, ascending to higher realms of existence, or merging with a larger universal consciousness.

The idea of the afterlife is often seen as a source of comfort and hope for many individuals, as it provides a sense of continuity and meaning beyond the limitations of our physical bodies. It also allows us to reconnect with loved ones who have departed and to continue our relationships with them on a spiritual level. I often tell clients that death is not the end of our journey; there is more to come when we depart these physical bodies.

While the nature of the soul and its existence beyond the physical world remains a mystery, the concept of the soul as eternal energy offers a transformative perspective on the nature of our being and our place in the universe. It reminds us that we are not limited to our physical bodies and that our journey continues beyond this material world.

"I can't control who comes through."

One of the critical features of mediumship is that the medium has no control over which spirits may come through during a reading. In other words, the medium cannot summon specific individuals or control the content of the communication. Instead, the spirits themselves choose to come through and convey messages to their loved ones. This lack of control on the medium's part is seen as evidence of the authenticity of the communication and the presence of a genuine spiritual connection.

Sometimes, someone may expect or even hope to hear from a loved one, and another comes through. It is not that the desired loved one is not present in the reading, but the soul who communicates may have the necessary information and messages to convey to provide sought-after healing, closure, and peace. For example, I had a reading with a young lady who was incredibly surprised that her father came through instead of her mom. The father first asked me to share an apology with her. He said he was sorry for being absent in her life and explained that many complications with drugs and alcohol prevented him from being the father he should have been to her. She began to cry and said she did not have a great relationship with him, and she confirmed that he did have a substance abuse problem. But, she said, although she was expecting her mom, who had recently passed, to come through, she did not realize how much she needed that apology from her dad and was glad his Spirit showed up. I advise my clients that Spirit may not give us what we want but will always give us what we need.

"Spirit communicates through signs and symbols."

Many spiritual and religious traditions suggest that the spirit world communicates with the living through signs and symbols. Mediums are thought to be able to interpret these signs and symbols and convey their meanings to those who seek to connect with the afterlife.

The signs and symbols of spirits can take many forms, ranging from visual and auditory experiences to more subtle sensations and feelings. For example, a soul may communicate through the appearance of a particular animal, a repeated number sequence, or a specific song or scent.

These signs and symbols are also often deeply personal and meaningful to the individual who receives them, and they are thought to convey messages of love, comfort, and guidance from the spirit world. For many, these signs and symbols offer comfort and connection with loved ones who have passed on and a reminder of the spiritual nature of existence.

While interpreting these signs and symbols is not an exact science, many mediums and spiritual practitioners argue that they can provide valuable insights into the spiritual realm and offer a sense of continuity and meaning beyond the physical world. By opening ourselves to the possibility of communication from the spirit world and paying attention to the signs and symbols around us, we can deepen our connection with the afterlife and better understand the mysteries of existence.

The signs and symbols spirits use to communicate through mediumship can take many forms and vary from person to person. However, here are a few common examples:

1. Animals: Spirit may use animals to communicate with their loved ones. For example, a butterfly or bird may repeatedly appear, representing a loved one who has passed on.

2. Numbers: Repeated sequences of numbers, such as 1111 or 444, may be used to communicate messages from the spirit world. These numbers may have personal significance to the individual receiving them or represent spiritual concepts such as unity or manifestation.

3. Scents: The sudden appearance of a particular scent, such as a perfume or flower, may signify that a loved one is present and attempting to communicate.

4. Dreams: Spirits may communicate through dreams, either directly or through symbolic imagery. Dreams may offer messages of comfort, guidance, or warning.

5. Music: A particular song or piece of music may have personal significance to an individual and be used as a means of communication from the spirit world.

6. Objects: Objects that have personal significance to an individual may suddenly appear or be moved differently, which could signify communication from the spirit world.

It is important to note that these signs and symbols may have different meanings for different individuals, and their interpretation of them can be subjective. Therefore, it is also essential to approach mediumship and the understanding of signs and symbols with an open mind and heart.

Finding a suitable medium for your spiritual needs

Step 1: Clarify Your Goals and Intentions

Before you start searching for a medium, take some time to reflect on what you hope to achieve through mediumship. Are you seeking guidance, healing, or closure? Understanding your intentions will help you find a medium with the appropriate expertise and abilities.

Step 2: Do Your Research

Begin your search by researching mediums in your area or online. You can use online directories, social media, or recommendations from friends and family. Look for reputable sources and check reviews or testimonials if available.

Step 3: Check Qualifications and Experience

Once you identify potential mediums, investigate their qualifications and experience. Ensure they have a good track record and inquire about their training or how long they've been practicing.

Step 4: Assess Their Specialty

Different mediums may specialize in various areas, such as connecting with departed loved ones, offering spiritual guidance, or energy healing. Choose a medium whose specialty aligns with your goals. If you are uncertain, feel free to ask the medium about their areas of expertise.

Step 5: Seek Recommendations

Do not hesitate to ask for references or testimonials from previous clients. Speaking with others who have worked with the medium can provide valuable insights into their abilities and effectiveness.

Step 6: Trust Your Intuition

Your gut feeling is a crucial factor in choosing the suitable medium. If something does not feel right or if you don't resonate with the medium's energy, it's okay to continue your search.

Step 7: Evaluate Costs and Logistics

Assess the medium's fees, session duration, and any necessary preparations for the session. Make sure the logistical aspects align with your budget and schedule.

Step 8: Book a Session

Book a session with the medium once you've researched and feel confident in your choice. Be open-minded and receptive during the experience, as it may provide the healing or guidance you seek.

Remember that finding the right medium is a personal journey, and choosing someone with whom you feel a strong connection and trust is essential. Taking the time to research and evaluate your options will help ensure a positive and meaningful experience.

We have just delved into the inner workings of mediumship, exploring the art, heart, and mechanics of this profound practice. We have learned that mediumship is a captivating and intricate way of communicating with the spirit world, bridging the physical and spiritual realms to deliver messages from departed loved ones. Through heightened awareness and the use of psychic faculties like clairvoyance, clairaudience, and clairsentience, mediums receive and transmit information from spirits. This process provides comfort, insight, and closure for those seeking connections with their departed loved ones. We have also discovered the two main types of mediums: physical mediums, who produce observable phenomena, and mental mediums, like me, who perceive and interpret messages from the spirit world through psychic faculties.

We have explored the fascinating concept that we do not "talk to the dead" but rather connect with souls that continue to exist as energy even after they depart from their physical bodies. This understanding challenges the conventional view of death, emphasizing the continuity of life beyond our earthly existence. By recognizing that we are beings of energy before, during, and after our physical lives, we gain a deeper understanding of our place in the universe and the interconnectedness of all living things.

The idea that we are energy before entering our bodies and will be energy once we depart from them speaks to the profound wisdom of many spiritual and philosophical traditions. It underscores the notion that our souls are eternal and indestructible, existing beyond time and space constraints. This belief provides solace and hope, affirming that our journey continues beyond the physical realm.

Another significant aspect of this chapter is the medium's lack of control over whose spirit comes through during a reading. This lack of control is a testament to the authenticity of mediumship, demonstrating that the spirits themselves choose to convey messages to their loved ones. Sometimes, unexpected spirits come forward, offering unexpected but significant messages that provide healing, closure, and peace. For example, a client could be set on receiving messages from a departed mother, but instead, their father comes through with a message they did not realize they needed for healing.

Furthermore, we have recognized that spirit communicates through signs and symbols. These signs, which can take various forms, including animals, numbers, scents, dreams, music, and objects, carry personal significance and serve as a means of connecting with the spirit world. By paying attention to these signs and symbols, we can deepen our connection with the afterlife and gain insight into the mysteries of existence.

Finally, you have a step-by-step guide to finding the perfect medium for your spiritual needs.

I hope this chapter has shed light on the profound nature of mediumship and the remarkable ways it can provide comfort, healing, and a sense of continuity with departed loved ones. It has expanded our understanding of the soul as eternal energy and the interconnectedness of all life forms. As we explore mediumship, we will continue to uncover the depths of this remarkable practice and its potential to illuminate the path of our spiritual journeys.

Chapter 4: Inner Workings: The Art, Heart, and Mechanics of Mediumship

Lesson: Understanding the Mechanics of Mediumship

In this lesson, we will dive into the inner workings of mediumship, exploring the mechanics and processes that facilitate communication with the spirit world.

- **Mechanics of Mediumship**: Gain insights into how mediumship operates, including the role of intuition, energy, and attunement to the spirit realm.

Exercise: Developing Your Intuition

1. Find a quiet, comfortable space to sit or lie down without distractions.
2. Close your eyes and take several deep breaths to center yourself.
3. Imagine a sphere of white light surrounding you, creating a protective and pure energy field.
4. Focus your attention on your heart center. Imagine a warm and radiant light emanating from this area.
5. Begin to trust your intuition by asking yourself simple questions. For example, ask, "What color is my aura today?" Pay attention to any immediate impressions or images that come to mind. Trust what you receive.
6. Practice this exercise regularly to strengthen your intuitive abilities. As you become more attuned to your intuition, you'll find connecting with the spirit realm easier.

Activity: Practice Connecting with a Departed Loved One

1. Choose a quiet and sacred space where you will not be disturbed.

2. Light a candle and take a moment to center yourself through deep breaths and relaxation.

3. Set the intention to connect with a departed loved one. You can say a prayer or affirmation to invite their presence.

4. Visualize the presence of your loved one in your mind's eye. Imagine them standing before you, radiating love and warmth.

5. Begin a conversation with them, either silently or out loud. Share your thoughts, feelings, and any messages you wish to convey.

6. Pay attention to any sensations, thoughts, or emotions that arise during this practice. Your loved one may communicate with you in subtle ways.

7. After your conversation, express gratitude for the connection and blow out the candle, closing the session.

This lesson aims to demystify the mechanics of mediumship, emphasizing the importance of intuition and energetic attunement. Developing your intuitive abilities and practicing connection exercises can enhance your mediumship skills and deepen your understanding of this profound art.

Chapter Five
Embracing The Invisible Thread:
The Deep Bond Between Grief and Mediumship

"Mediumship can provide a bridge between this world and the next, offering hope and comfort to those who are grieving."
~ **Theresa Caputo**

Nijah's Story

It was a warm and sunny day when Nijah first entered my office. She had flown from Jacksonville, Florida, to Atlanta, Georgia, because she wanted an in-person reading. I assured her the energy would be the same over the phone or by video, but she insisted on meeting me and doing it face-to-face. Nijah's energy was a mixture of excitement and nervousness. She paced the floor as I gave her my spiel about how the session worked. Finally, I nodded gently and invited her to sit down as I prepared to bridge the gap between our world and the spirit realm.

The first question I asked was if she was there for the young man who had passed. Her eyes instantly swelled up with tears, and she said, "Yes, it's my son, and I miss him so much, and I just...I need to know he's all right." My heart ached for her, and I knew the connection between grief and mediumship would be crucial in our session.

As a medium, I have the privilege of helping countless individuals find solace and healing, but something about Nijah's story resonated deep within me. As I closed my eyes and reached out to the spirit world, I could feel Nijah's son drawing near. The warmth of his love for his mother enveloped me, and I could sense his deep longing to offer comfort and reassurance. I took a deep breath and began to relay her message.

"Nijah, your son shows me that he was murdered. Sitting in a car, someone ambushed him. He knew who the person was. He also showed me that he was into music, a rapper. He is making me hear this rap song by Jay Z and Eminem called *Renegade*." She gasped and said, "Dr. Foster, he was a rapper, and the last song he recorded and let me listen to right before he died was titled *Renegade*." I was floored, and so was she. I am always amazed at the messages Spirit brings to confirm their presence with us. I continued, "He knows you are devastated by his passing but does not want you to grieve yourself into sickness or death. He assures you his soul is fine and that he will greet you when you cross into the heavenly realm." "He wants you to know how incredibly proud he is of you. He has been watching over you and sees the strength and courage you have shown in the face of this devastating loss," I said.

Tears began streaming down Nijah's face, and I knew that this message had touched a place deep within her heart. The bond between Nijah and her son became even more evident as our session continued. Their love transcended life's and death's boundaries, offering comfort and hope during this challenging time.

By the end of our time together, Nijah was visibly more at peace, her heart a little lighter. As she left my office, she whispered, "Thank you. Thank you for helping me feel close to my son again."

As I sat alone in my office that day, I was again reminded of the deep and powerful bond between grief and mediumship. It is a sacred and emotional connection that allows us to reach beyond the veil of life and death, offering solace and healing to grieving people. Through this energetic connection, we can feel the presence of our loved ones, even as we learn to navigate the complex journey of loss and mourning. As a medium, I am honored to serve as a conduit for these connections.

The Power of The Invisible Thread

Grief is a powerful force that can shake us to our core and leave us feeling lost and alone. It is a natural response to loss and a necessary healing process. Many people do not realize that grief is also a doorway to the spiritual realm. Through grief, we can connect with those who have passed on and find solace in the invisible thread that weaves grief and mediumship together.

As a spiritual teacher and medium, I have seen firsthand the power of this invisible thread. I have witnessed the transformation when we embrace our grief and open ourselves up to the messages and wisdom from the other side. But embracing this invisible thread requires courage and a willingness to face our pain head-on. It needs us to be vulnerable and open to the unknown. It requires us to trust in the power of love and the unbreakable bonds that connect us all.

Through my work as a medium, I understand that the invisible thread that weaves grief and mediumship together is not something to be feared but something to be embraced. It reminds us that our loved ones are never truly gone but are always with us in spirit. When we hold onto the unbreakable bond that we share with our loved ones, we allow ourselves to heal and move forward in a way that demonstrates our admiration for and love for them. As a result, we can discover serenity and comprehension amid our anguish and express gratitude for the precious gift of life that we have been blessed with.

The invisible thread that weaves grief and mediumship together is a powerful reminder of the spiritual nature of our existence. It reminds us that we are never truly alone and that love transcends even death. We can find healing, understanding, and a deep sense of peace amid our grief by embracing this.

The Sacred Space of Mediumship

We all know that grief is a natural part of life and that losing someone we love can be unbearable. Yet, as we journey through this challenging terrain, we must also recognize the divine potential for healing and growth that lies within. Therefore, I want to share the profound truth of mediumship. This spiritual practice can serve as a healing bridge between the living and the departed, offering comfort, connection, and a pathway to wholeness even in the face of unspeakable loss.

When we open ourselves to the power of mediumship, we enter a sacred space where the veil between the physical and the spiritual realms is at its thinnest. In this sacred space, our loved ones who have crossed over can reach out to us, offering messages of love, guidance, and reassurance. Through mediumship, we can forge a soulful connection with our departed loved ones, finding solace in knowing that love transcends the boundaries of life and death.

Mediumship is a sacred space that connects the physical and spiritual realms. It is a space where those who have passed on can communicate with those still on Earth. It is a space that allows for healing, closure, and understanding. I have been blessed to witness firsthand the power of this sacred space. I have seen its impact on individuals struggling with losing a loved one. I have seen the healing that occurs when a message is received from someone who has passed on.

But mediumship is not just about receiving messages from the other side. It is about creating a safe and loving space where those passed on feel heard and understood. It is about respecting the boundaries of the physical and spiritual realms and honoring the sacredness of the connection being made. It is vital to approach this sacred space with humility, respect, and a deep sense of purpose. It is not something to be taken lightly or used for personal gain. Instead, it is a space that demands reverence and an unwavering commitment to the highest good of all involved. I have found that the more I honor the sacredness of this space, the more profound and meaningful the connections become. It reminds us that there is so much more to this life than what we can see with our physical eyes. And it is a testament to the power of love and the unbreakable bonds that connect us all, even in death. As a medium, I am honored to hold space for those who have passed on and witness the healing and transformation within this sacred space.

The Power of Spirit Communication

When we receive messages from our loved ones in the spirit world, we often find that these communications carry with them a profound sense of love and healing. Whether it is a simple word of reassurance, a shared memory, or a message of guidance, the Spirit world seeks to uplift and support us during our grief.

For example, consider the story of a woman named Natasha who lost her husband suddenly. Devastated and seeking answers, she sought my help to connect with her husband's spirit. During the reading, I shared a message from Natasha's husband that he was at peace and that he would always be with her in spirit. In addition, I communicated with her other things about their family that brought her confirmation. Still, one thing she admitted was the undeniable proof that it was her husband's spirit communicating with us. He told me to bring up "the black hat," and she would know what it meant. I did, and Natasha burst into tears. When she gained composure, she said her husband was wearing a black hat when he died, and she kept the hat on her headrest in her car as a reminder that he is always with her and always had her back. She admitted to being a little skeptical of mediumship before the reading but that a tiny, yet hugely significant, detail confirmed his spiritual presence. This simple message comforted Natasha and helped her find the strength to move forward, knowing her husband's love would always be with her.

As we explore the healing power of mediumship, it is important to remember that this spiritual practice is not about replacing the grief process but rather about supporting and nurturing our healing journey. By embracing the comfort and connection that mediumship offers, we can begin to find our way back to wholeness, learning to live our lives in harmony with both the seen and the unseen.

I invite you to open to the healing bridge connecting you with your departed loved ones and offer support, guidance, and a pathway to wholeness. In this sacred space, we can learn to live in balance, honoring the pain of loss and the love that endures beyond life and death.

Chapter 5: Embracing the Invisible Thread: The Deep Bond Between Grief and Mediumship

Lesson: Exploring the Connection Between Grief and Mediumship

In this lesson, we will delve into the profound connection between grief and mediumship, understanding how they intersect and influence one another.

- **Grief and Mediumship**: Explore the intricate relationship between grief and mediumship, recognizing how grief can open pathways to connecting with the spirit world.

Exercise: Identifying Signs and Messages from Loved Ones

1. Take some quiet time to reflect on your experiences since losing your loved one. Have you noticed any signs or messages that may have come from them? These could be symbolic, such as a specific song on the radio or a recurring dream.

2. Keep a journal dedicated to these signs and messages. Document each occurrence, noting the date, time, and circumstances.

3. Reflect on the patterns or symbols that repeat in these messages. Are there common themes or images? Please pay attention to your intuition as you interpret their meaning.

4. Share your observations with a trusted friend or support group. Sometimes, others can offer valuable insights or validations.

Activity: Create a Symbolic Collage of Your Connection with Loved Ones

1. Gather magazines, images, and art supplies such as scissors, glue, and a poster board or canvas.

2. Sit in a quiet and reflective space. Take a few deep breaths to center yourself.

3. Begin flipping through the magazines and selecting images, words, or phrases that resonate with your connection to your departed loved ones. Trust your intuition as you choose them.

4. Assemble these chosen elements onto your poster board or canvas, creating a collage representing the bond and communication you share with your loved ones in the spirit world.

5. Allow your creative process to flow without judgment. Your collage doesn't need to be perfect; it should reflect your emotions and experiences.

6. Display your symbolic collage where you can see it regularly. It serves as a reminder of the ongoing connection with your loved ones.

This lesson explores the deep bond between grief and mediumship, recognizing that grief can be a powerful gateway to connecting with the spirit realm. By identifying signs and messages and creating a symbolic collage, you can acknowledge and embrace the invisible thread that continues to bind you to your departed loved ones.

Chapter Six

The Myth of Untimely Death: Sacred Contracts and Soul's Knowing

"Soul contracts are the cosmic agreements that shape our destiny, reminding us that every experience has a purpose, and every relationship holds a lesson."

~ **Dr. Lakara Foster**

Maria's Story

Maria sat nervously in my office, her heart heavy with grief and longing. She had come to me seeking solace and closure after the tragic loss of her dear friend, Alex. As Maria explained, Alex had been taken from this world "far too soon" in a devastating car accident, leaving Maria and their circle of friends shattered and full of unanswered questions.

As I entered the room, her calming presence enveloped Maria like a warm embrace. Sensing Maria's anguish, I smiled gently and held her hands. "Maria, I understand the pain you carry in your heart. I will do my best to help you find the answers you seek."

With hope and trepidation, Maria opened up, sharing memories of Alex, the vibrant soul who had brought joy and laughter to their lives. She spoke of their last conversation, plans, and the void his passing had left behind.

As I closed my eyes, stillness settled in the room. I took a deep breath, allowing my connection to the spirit world to guide me. Maria's heart raced in the silence, unsure of what to expect.

Suddenly, I said. "Alex is here, Maria. He is ready to communicate with us."

Tears welled up in Maria's eyes as she felt excitement and trepidation. "Alex?" she whispered, her voice filled with longing.

Alex's presence began to manifest. His comforting and familiar energy enveloped the room. A wave of emotion washed over Maria as she felt the essence of her beloved friend.

Alex's spirit began to communicate, and I became a vessel for this interaction. I shared with Maria information that she quickly confirmed. One of the most profound things Alex wanted Maria to know was that his transition was not "untimely." It was part of a greater plan that unfolded to protect others.

Maria listened intently, tears streaming down her face. "What do you mean? How could his passing be part of a plan?"

Alex's spirit explained, "That night, after the party, I found myself in a predicament. I did not want to risk driving home tipsy, so I ordered an

Uber. Little did I know that this choice would intersect with the path of a drunk driver. The collision was a tragic event but not an accident in the grand scheme."

Maria's mind reeled with a mix of disbelief and acceptance. "Is he saying that it was meant for him to transition that night?" Alex's spirit responded gently, "Yes, it was my time to transition, and my passing served a purpose greater than our human understanding can grasp. In leaving this world, I became a catalyst for awareness for change. My story serves as a reminder of the dangers of drunk driving and the importance of making responsible choices. It was not untimely, but rather a part of the intricate web of life's interconnectedness."

Maria's heart ached as she absorbed Alex's words. The pain of loss still lingered, but a glimmer of understanding began to emerge. She could now see the threads of purpose and meaning in his passing.

Maria and Alex's spirit shared their final exchange in the following moments. He assured her of his continued presence, offering guidance and love from the realm beyond. He reminded her of the beauty of their friendship and the joy they had shared.

As Maria left the reading, her heart carried a newfound perspective. She understood that all our lives are part of a bigger plan. One that we agree to even before we enter the physical world. So, while she still fills the void of the loss of Alex, she can still rejoice in the fact that his soul contract is complete, and he is at peace.

Sacred Contracts

In the wake of profound loss, families may grapple with the concept of untimely death and questions of more profound significance. As they seek solace and understanding, they may embark on a journey to explore the notion of spiritual contracts and the soul's awareness of its entry and departure from the physical body.

A deep truth lies beyond earthly sorrows, where the boundary between realms is faint. This truth dispels the illusion of untimely death. In this space, souls transcend time and space, journeying purposefully. When they start their human lives, they engage in a sacred dialogue with the universe, forging contracts that guide their path, define their purpose, and shape their destiny.

These sacred contracts are not arbitrary or random. They are crafted with intention, love, and a deep understanding of the soul's growth and evolution. Each soul enters this world with a blueprint—a plan encompassing its unique journey, the relationships it will forge, and the lessons it will learn. In this grand existence, every life is intertwined, every connection purposeful.

As souls descend into the physical realm, they carry with them a deep knowing—an intrinsic awareness of their appointed arrival and parting time. They understand that the measure of life cannot be confined to its duration but rather to the profound impact it makes upon the hearts and minds of others. I tell clients often that while we cannot control the quantity of our years, we certainly have control over the quality of our years.

In the face of heart-wrenching loss, when the weight of grief threatens to consume us, it is easy to question the fairness of timing. But in these moments of darkness, we must summon the courage to embrace a higher truth surpassing human comprehension's boundaries.

We are freed from the shackles of despair when we recognize that there is no such thing as an untimely death. However fleeting, we are reminded that every life carries a purpose beyond our limited understanding. The souls we mourn have completed their sacred contracts, having fulfilled their obligations to the universe.

When we grieve, it is natural to yearn for the presence of our loved ones, to ache for their physical embrace. Yet, if we open our hearts to the whispers of the soul, we may find comfort in knowing that their essence continues to guide and inspire us.

The signs are subtle and profound—a gentle touch upon the cheek, a whispered word upon the wind, a synchronistic encounter that defies explanation. These are the reminders that our departed loved ones are not truly gone but have transitioned to a realm where their spirit shines eternally.

The departure of these individuals is a sign of how perfectly a divine force orchestrates life. Their souls were conscious of their predetermined time and decided to come to the physical world to fulfill a purpose beyond our human understanding. Even though they are no longer physically present, their influence remains, leaving a lasting imprint on the collective mind of humanity.

The Soul's Knowing

Deep within the core of our being, there is a timeless and boundless soul that carries the wisdom of lifetimes and the memories of our eternal journey. This soul is intricately connected to the divine source and holds within it the imprints of countless lifetimes and the lessons learned through each incarnation. By tapping into this inherent wisdom, we can bring healing and enlightenment.

The soul knows that our existence extends far beyond this current lifetime. It remembers the adventures of previous lives, the joys and sorrows, the triumphs and tribulations. It carries the accumulated wisdom, etched in its very essence, ready to guide us on our path of growth and transformation.

As we embark on our human journey, we may find ourselves caught in the web of forgetfulness, losing touch with the profound truths our soul carries. Yet, fragments of this wisdom often surface in moments of intuition, in the flashes of insight that seem to come from a place more profound than the conscious mind. We catch glimpses of what our soul truly knows and remembers in these moments.

As human beings, we are all interconnected, and our souls remember this fact. Every relationship and encounter that we have serves a purpose and holds meaning. Our souls recognize a divine thread that connects us all and encourages us to learn from one another. These lessons help us grow and evolve as individuals. Our souls also remember our true purpose and our unique gifts and talents. They guide us towards paths that align with our soul's calling, urging us to express our true selves and contribute to the world. Our souls remind us of our passions, aspirations, and the service we are here to offer to the world.

The soul knows that love is the essence of our being. It reminds us that we are born from love, and to love, we shall return. It reminds us of the eternal bonds we share with those we hold dear, transcending the boundaries of time and space. It knows that love is the most significant force in the universe, and its power can heal, transform, and illuminate even the darkest moments.

During profound reflection moments, when we fully embrace the quietness within, we can perceive the gentle whispers of our souls. By connecting with this inner wisdom, we can make decisions and take actions that align with our true selves. To create a space where the voice of our soul can be heard, we can engage in practices like meditation, journaling, and introspection. Through this connection with our soul, we find comfort and direction in times of uncertainty and loss.

The soul remembers the lessons we learned from our departed loved ones and their profound impact on our lives. It carries their love and wisdom, inviting us to honor their legacy by embodying the qualities they cherished most.

In embracing our soul's knowing, we align ourselves with the divine flow of life. We awaken to the truth that we are more than our physical bodies, more than our transient experiences. We are divine beings on a journey of expansion and remembrance. Let us embark on this sacred journey, honoring the wisdom within and embracing the soul's knowing and remembering. And in doing so, may we uncover the profound depths of our being, living in alignment with our soul's purpose and creating a life of fulfillment, love, and deep connection.

Chapter 6: The Myth of Untimely Death: Sacred Contracts and A Soul's Knowing

Lesson: Understanding the Concept of Sacred Contracts

In this lesson, we will explore the concept of sacred contracts, which play a significant role in understanding our life's purpose and experiences.

- **Sacred Contracts**: Delve into the idea that our souls enter into agreements or contracts before incarnating on Earth, shaping our life's path and lessons.

Exercise: Reflecting on Your Life's Lessons

1. Find a quiet and contemplative space to reflect without distractions.
2. Take out a journal or a notebook and pen.
3. Consider the significant events and experiences in your life, especially those related to loss and grief. Write down these events.
4. Reflect on the lessons or insights you have gained from each event. How have these experiences shaped you as a person? What wisdom have they imparted?
5. Think about the people who have played significant roles in your life, especially those who have passed away. How have their presence and absence influenced your journey?
6. Take your time with this exercise and be open to the emotions that may arise during your reflections.

Activity: Write a Letter to a Loved One About Your Spiritual Journey

1. Choose one of your departed loved ones with whom you connected significantly.

2. Find a quiet and sacred space to sit comfortably.

3. Begin writing a letter to your chosen loved one. Share your spiritual journey, lessons, and how their presence or absence has influenced your path.

4. Express your emotions, thoughts, and gratitude. You can also ask questions or seek guidance.

5. After writing the letter, take a moment to meditate or reflect silently. Be open to any intuitive insights or sensations.

6. Keep this letter as a personal keepsake; if you feel comfortable, you can burn it as a symbolic act of sending your message to the spirit realm.

This lesson invites you to explore the concept of sacred contracts to help you understand how the experiences and lessons in your life, especially those related to loss, are part of a larger spiritual journey. By reflecting on your life's lessons and writing a letter to a loved one, you can deepen your understanding of the soul's knowledge and the wisdom that comes from it.

Chapter Seven

The Wisdom of Spirit:
Lessons from Beyond the Veil

"When the student is ready, the teacher will appear."
~ **Buddha**

Hakim's Story

As I welcomed Hakim into my reading space, I could sense the anticipation and excitement radiating from him. He was eager to connect with his late grandmother, a well-known religious leader who had left an indelible mark on the world through her teachings and guidance. I could tell that Hakim's bond with his grandmother was powerful, and I felt honored to facilitate their connection.

We began the reading, and I focused on inviting Hakim's grandmother to join us. I felt her warm and loving presence almost immediately, and I knew, despite what Hakim may have assumed, that she was eager to communicate with her grandson.

I told Hakim, "Your grandmother is here with us, and she's filled with so much love and joy at seeing you. I have a feeling you are one of her favorites."

Hakim's eyes filled with tears as he replied, "I've missed her so much." Then, he cheekily added, "Of course I am," and we laughed.

I took a deep breath and began describing the images that his grandmother showed me. I informed Hakim that I saw a church and that she was essential to this church and the religious community. He confirmed what I saw and said, "Yes, she was!" I emphasized, "Hakim, she is a significant person, and I am seeing something named in her honor." Hakim smiled and excitedly said, "Yes, there is a street named for her in our hometown!"

Feeling enthusiastic by the confirmations that were coming in, I listened more intently as his grandmother's message continued to come through. I continued, "She wants you to know she loves you and has been watching over you. She also mentioned something about religion. It seems like she wants to share a particular message with you about that. She wants to talk about religion and the afterlife." I was unsure what Hakim would say about the subsequent revelation that Spirit gave as it stunned me even to hear it as a Minister, but I knew I had to deliver the message exactly how Spirit was giving it. So, I paused and quietly said, "Your grandmother said there is no religion in heaven."

Hakim looked surprised and asked, "What does she mean by that? She was such a devout believer in her faith."

I continued to relay his grandmother's message. "She is telling me that the spirit world transcends the boundaries of religious doctrine. In heaven, all souls are united by the divine light of love that connects them. It's a place where everyone is welcomed and embraced, regardless of their religious beliefs, and that love is the essence of all existence."

As I shared this message, I saw Hakim processing this new information. It was clear that this revelation was both unexpected and comforting for him. He responded, "That's such a beautiful message. It is not what I expected to hear because she was such a devout Christian, and I long thought our religious beliefs played a role in our experiences in the afterlife."

I shared with Hakim that that is a common belief. Still, his grandmother wanted to emphasize that the true nature of heaven and the spirit world is much broader and more inclusive than any single religion can encompass. So, I encouraged him, "She wants you to find comfort in knowing that she is in a place of love and harmony, surrounded by the divine light that unites all souls."

Hakim responded, "Lakara, that is a beautiful message. Knowing she is in a place of love and peace is comforting. I will remember all this as I navigate my spiritual journey. To have her show up in this reading makes me feel closer to her and more connected to something greater."

As we concluded the reading, Hakim left with a sense of peace and a newfound understanding of the interconnectedness of all souls. It was an honor to witness his journey of healing and growth, and I felt grateful to be a part of it.

Over the years, Spirit has been the most patient and excellent teacher and has taught me profound lessons. Through countless communications with the spirit world, I have been blessed to receive insights that have not only transformed my life but also guided many others on their path to healing and spiritual growth. In addition to Spirit sharing with me that there is no religion in heaven, we'll explore three other essential lessons from Spirit world that have changed my perspective: "Death is not a punishment," "Death is an illusion," and "There is only heaven," and I will also share a channeled message I received from Spirit at the end of this chapter.

Death is not a punishment.

One benefit to being a medium is that I learn just as much from Spirit as the people to whom I give readings. One of the most critical lessons Spirit has taught me is that death is not a punishment or something to be feared. Instead, it is a natural part of the soul's journey, transitioning from one state of existence to another. When we can view death in this light, we can release the fear and anxiety that often accompany the grieving process, allowing us to embrace the beauty and growth that come from the loss experience. Many people feel guilty or responsible for the death of their loved ones, and they may think that their loved ones are being punished for something they did. This can lead to feelings of shame, regret, and self-blame, making the grieving process even more difficult.

When someone passes away, it is not because they have done something wrong or are being punished. Death is a natural part of life and not something anyone can control. It is something we all must eventually face. I believe we sign a soul contract before entering these physical bodies. This contract is an agreement we make with The Creator/The Universe/The God of our understanding. It stipulates when we will be conceived, when we will be born, and when we depart these physical bodies. This contract also specifies our purpose and who and what will be necessary for us to carry it out. The beautiful part of this contract is that we design it when we are mere souls. Before we arrive in our earthly bodies, we agree to forget, and being born ignites the process of remembering. Have you ever wondered why certain people, places, and situations feel so familiar? It is because we had planned the journey ahead of time, even down to when and how we would leave when we were done.

The idea of death is so painful for us that we rarely discuss it or even plan for it. When a loved one transitions, it catches us off guard and sometimes arrests our social, relational, emotional, and professional development. We find ourselves stuck and unable to move past our loved ones leaving us. I find that often it is not just that the person passed, but also how they passed and whether there is closure when they pass.

When individuals understand that death is not a punishment, they can begin to let go of feelings of guilt and self-blame. They can also find comfort in knowing their loved ones are at peace and still energetically present with them. This understanding can bring a sense of closure and healing to grieving individuals and help them move forward. It can also bring healing and peace to individuals struggling with guilt and self-blame. Finally, by embracing the natural cycle of life and understanding that our loved ones are still with us somehow, we can find comfort and healing amid our grief.

The topic of death is sensitive and can be challenging to comprehend. We often associate it with feelings of loss and sadness. But as we explore our spirituality and recognize our connection to the divine, we understand death as a natural part of our spiritual growth. It is a necessary step in our journey toward enlightenment and something we should embrace without fear.

Death is an Illusion

Another powerful lesson from Spirit is the understanding that death is an illusion. As a spiritual teacher and coach, I understand that death is not an absolute end but a transition from one state of being to another. Although our loved ones' physical bodies may no longer be with us, their spirit's essence remains. While our physical bodies may cease to function, our souls continue to exist, carrying the essence of who we are into the next phase of our journey. By recognizing that our connections with our loved ones are never truly severed, we can maintain a sense of hope and comfort, even in the face of profound loss. And when we embrace this understanding, we can find peace and comfort in even the most difficult times. We can trust the universe and the divine plan unfolding for us.

The concept of death as an illusion is rooted in the idea that all that exists is energy. Energy is neither created nor destroyed; it simply changes form. This is the first law of thermodynamics, also known as the law of energy conservation. Therefore, our energy does not disappear when we die but transforms into a new form. This is why many people believe in reincarnation, the idea that the soul or consciousness continues to exist in a new form after death. It is important to remember that death is not something that happens to us but something that happens for us. It allows us to shed our physical form and move on to the next phase of our spiritual journey. When we view death as a natural part of life, we see beauty in everything. We can appreciate the present moment and live our lives with a greater sense of purpose and fulfillment.

Many people ponder what happens to us after we die. If we consider death a transitional phase, it is believed that our consciousness continues to exist in a different form. This form could be reincarnation, where our soul is reborn into a new body, or an afterlife, where our consciousness persists in a non-physical realm.

The idea of an afterlife is supported by near-death experiences (NDEs), where people report having profound spiritual experiences when they are clinically dead. These experiences often involve a feeling of peace, a sense of being surrounded by loved ones who have passed away, and a profound understanding of the nature of the Universe.

Death is not an end but a new beginning. It is a transformation we must all go through at some point in our lives. Let us embrace the mystery of death with open hearts and minds and trust in the universe and the divine plan unfolding for us. May we live our lives with purpose, passion, and love.

There is Only Heaven

What if I told you that there is only heaven and that hell does not exist, at least not in the way we have been instructed biblically? That is undoubtedly one of the lessons Spirit has taught me. Throughout many readings, Spirit has communicated that Heaven is not a physical place but a state of consciousness. It is a place of infinite love, compassion, and joy where we are connected to the divine and each other profoundly and meaningfully. In Heaven, there is no judgment, punishment, or fear. There is only love and compassion.

This understanding of heaven is not limited to any one religious tradition. Instead, it is a universal concept that transcends all boundaries and is available to everyone regardless of their beliefs or background.

As someone who guides others on their spiritual journey, I understand that the idea of hell can be scary and unsettling. The concept of hell has long been a source of fear and anxiety for many people. We are often taught that if we do not live according to a particular set of rules, we will be punished eternally in a place of darkness and suffering. However, I genuinely believe heaven is a state of being open to everyone, regardless of their beliefs or background. My experiences with spirit have shown me that heaven is a place of love, peace, and unity beyond what we see in our physical reality. It is a place where our souls can find rest and healing, free from the challenges and limitations of our earthly existence. Embracing this belief can bring great comfort, especially when we think of our loved ones who have passed on. They are surrounded by love and light; someday, we will join them in this eternal embrace. When we let go of the fear of hell and embrace the idea of heaven, we can live our lives with a greater sense of peace and joy. We can focus on creating a better world for ourselves and future generations and support each other in our spiritual journeys.

I am often asked, "Well, what happens to people who live 'bad' lives if heaven is all there is?" It is a common question that deserves a thoughtful and compassionate answer.

First, it is essential to understand that heaven is not a reward or punishment for how we live our lives. It is not where good people go, and bad people are excluded. Instead, it is a state of consciousness available to all of us.

When we transition from this life to the next, we are met with the love and compassion of the divine. We can reflect on our lives and learn from good and bad experiences.

For those who may have lived a "bad" life, this is an opportunity for growth and transformation. They are not punished but instead given a chance to learn from their mistakes, make amends for any harm they may have caused, and decide if they want to do it all over again as a different person.

It is also essential to understand that our actions in this life do have consequences. If we live in a way that harms others, we will experience the results of those actions. This may include guilt or regret and the need to make amends. We may even experience karma for the misdeeds we commit. But even in the face of these consequences, we are never excluded from the love and compassion of the divine. We can always learn, grow, and move towards a greater sense of peace and joy.

So, if you are worried about what will happen to those who live immoral lives, know that they are not punished eternally. Instead, they can learn and grow, just as we all are.

So, let us embrace the idea that there is no hell, only heaven. Let us focus on love and compassion and work towards creating a world where everyone can experience the joy and beauty of heaven. Let us also accept the idea of heaven as a state of consciousness that is available to all of us. We should focus on love and compassion and on living our lives in a way that brings joy and peace to ourselves and those around us and let us trust in the infinite love and compassion of the divine, knowing that we are all worthy of eternal love and acceptance, no matter what we may have done in our lives.

The wisdom of Spirit has the power to transform our lives, offering us a renewed perspective on the nature of death and the connections we share with our loved ones. By embracing these lessons from beyond the veil, we can release the fear and pain that often accompany loss, allowing ourselves to heal and grow in the light of love and understanding.

Remember, knowing that our journey through grief is not solitary, we are guided and supported by the eternal wisdom of spirit, and together, we can find the strength to emerge from the darkness and into the light.

Channeled Message from Spirit

"Death is not the end. Death is not failure. Death is not a punishment. We do not lose to death. It cannot win, nor is it seeking to defeat life. It is simply the gateway or door to eternal life, eternal living, and reuniting with God in pure form, absent of the physical body. We will all walk through that door as there is no way for the soul to rejoin God/ oneness/ universal consciousness except through that divine portal. So, while you are rightfully mourning the loss of the physical presence of loved ones, I pray that you find an inkling of joy in the revelation that our lives continue as spirit energy here to assist as ancestors and that God is still using us to build up the Kingdom of Heaven.

We all have a nonnegotiable date when we will walk through the portal that we have collectively agreed to call death, and on that day, we will reunite with our departed loved ones and God. Until then, you will undoubtedly grieve to some degree, as suffering is on the spectrum of the human experience. However, as the ones that have gone before you, we do not want you to grieve yourselves to the point that you are not continuing to live out the fullness of your humanity, and part of that means experiencing heaven on Earth. We have discovered on the other side that we are in heaven, but more importantly, you do not have to die to experience this realm. It is why you were given a body in the first place. So, choose today to experience the state of consciousness we call heaven by loving all you meet unconditionally, walking in forgiveness, counting it all joy, releasing egoic fear and anxiety, ceasing to compare yourselves and your lives to others, accepting and loving your gifts and taking care of your earthly temple because while you can't control the number of your years, you can certainly control the quality, and spending time in nature and being wowed by the goodness and greatness of God."- Spirit

Chapter 7: The Wisdom of Spirit: Lessons from Beyond the Veil

Lesson: Learning from Messages Received

In this lesson, we will explore the invaluable wisdom that can be gained from messages received during mediumship experiences.

- **Messages from Beyond**: Discover how the messages received during mediumship can provide guidance, healing, and a deeper understanding of life and the afterlife.

Exercise: Journaling Your Mediumship Experiences

1. Dedicate a journal specifically for documenting your mediumship experiences. Choose one that resonates with you, perhaps with calming colors or spiritual motifs.

2. Whenever you have a mediumship session or encounter signs and messages from the spirit world, write down the date, time, and details of the experience. Be as descriptive as possible.

3. Reflect on your feelings and emotions during the experience. How did it make you feel? Did any insights or revelations come to you?

4. Document any specific messages or information you received from departed loved ones or spiritual entities. Include any symbols or imagery that appeared.

5. Use this journal to make sense of your mediumship encounters. It can serve as a valuable resource for your spiritual growth.

Activity: Share Your Mediumship Experience with a Supportive Friend

1. Reach out to a close and supportive friend or family member who is open to discussing spiritual topics.

2. Choose a comfortable and quiet space to meet with your chosen confidant.

3. Share one of your mediumship experiences from your journal. Be open and honest about your thoughts, feelings, and any doubts or questions that arose during the encounter.

4. Encourage your friend to listen with an open heart and mind, offering their insights or reflections if they feel inclined.

5. After sharing, take some time to discuss the experience together. Your friend may provide a different perspective or offer comforting words.

6. Express gratitude to your friend for their support and understanding.

Sharing your mediumship experiences with a trusted friend can be a profoundly enriching and validating experience. It allows you to connect with others with similar experiences or provides a space to express your thoughts and emotions about your encounters with the spirit world.

Chapter Eight
I Hope You Dance:
Opening Your Heart Again to Love

"I hope you still feel small when you stand beside the ocean.
Whenever one door closes, I hope one more opens,
Promise me that you will give faith a fighting chance,
And when you get the choice to sit it out or dance,
I hope you dance."
~ **LeeAnn Womack**

Kimberly's Story

Kimberly's husband died unexpectedly. I knew this because I saw Spirit "snap their fingers," which is my sign indicating that the person died suddenly or unexpectedly and usually without the chance to say goodbye. Kimberly confirmed that he transitioned from a heart attack in his sleep several months before her reading. Even though her husband Jay came through with beautiful confirmations, a year later, Kimber still struggled to find a way forward and wondered if she would ever be happy again. She and Jay were high school sweethearts, married for 30 years, and shared five children. She could not stop crying, and I witnessed the depth of her pain and the rawness of her grief.

Kimberly explained, "I had hoped that the medium reading would bring me comfort and clarity, but I still find myself stuck in this overwhelming sadness. I do not know how to move forward." I told Kimberly, "Grief is a complicated journey with no linear path, so it is common to still feel a deep ache even after connecting with your husband through mediumship. Remember, the reading was a glimpse into your eternal bond, but it does not instantly erase the pain. Moving forward is a gradual process that requires patience, self-compassion, and a willingness to honor the complexities of your emotions. Allow yourself to feel what you feel without judgment."

Kimberly responded, "That's the thing, Dr. Foster. I feel like I am betraying my husband's memory when I even think about moving forward. How can I honor him while still finding a way to live and love again?"

I exclaimed, "Your love for your husband is eternal and will always be a part of you." I told her, "Moving forward does not diminish the love you shared; it is an opportunity to honor his memory by embracing the precious gift of life. Remember, love is not finite. You can carry your love for your husband while opening yourself to new connections. Trust that he will want you to find joy and fulfillment again. You honor his legacy by living authentically and nurturing love within your own life."

I knew Kimberly heard me, but it would take a while before the words could penetrate her being. Finally, she said, "It is challenging even to imagine finding joy again, but deep down, I know he would want me to be happy. How do I begin to rebuild my life without feeling guilty?

I reminded her that guilt is a natural companion on the path of grief, but it is essential to remember that guilt serves no purpose in healing. It would be best to allow yourself to feel the emotions as they arise, including guilt, but gently release them. I encouraged Kimberly to cultivate self-compassion to understand that she is human and navigating a complex journey and to practice forgiveness, both for herself and her husband. I advised her that he would never want her to carry the weight of guilt. She can honor his memory and their love by healing and finding joy.

Kimberly asked, "How can I find the strength to take that first step toward rebuilding my life?" I shared with her that the strength to take that first step begins with self-nurturing and self-discovery. It is vital to allow oneself the grace of time and reflection and to engage in practices that support your healing, such as journaling, meditation, or seeking the guidance of a grief counselor. Surround yourself with a supportive community that can hold space for your journey. As you gradually find moments of solace and clarity, trust your intuition. It will guide you toward the opportunities and possibilities that resonate with your soul. Remember, you have within you the power to rise and rebuild, one step at a time.

Kimberly said, "Dr. Foster, your words have brought me comfort and hope. I know the road ahead will not be easy, but I am grateful for your guidance and the reminder that I can honor my husband while finding my way to live and love again."

Love Will Go On

Some clients find themselves yearning for companionship with time. They may long deeply for love and intimacy following the profound loss of a loved one. Seeking new love after such a loss can be intricate. It is a journey filled with hope and trepidation, a delicate balance between honoring the past and embracing future possibilities. The echoes of your beloved may linger within you, and it is essential to celebrate the love you shared, the cherished memories, and the lessons from that sacred union. Realize that love is not something left behind but carried within, like a precious gem in your soul.

As you embark on this journey, allow yourself to experience the full range of emotions that arise. Grieve the loss and acknowledge fears when opening your heart to love again. Be kind to yourself, for healing takes time and patience, and remember that seeking new love does not mean replacing what was lost but expanding your capacity for love and connection. It is an invitation to discover your resilience, ability to love again, and courage to embrace life's blessings. Navigating this path requires embracing vulnerability. It is natural to fear getting hurt again or repeating past mistakes but consider releasing the need for control and trust in life's flow. Believe that the Universe, in its infinite wisdom, will guide you toward new love and companionship.

When seeking new love, be mindful of your intentions. Examine your motives to ensure you are not seeking mere distraction or an escape from grief. Approach new relationships with a genuine desire for connection, growth, and mutual support. Seek a partner who understands and respects your journey, embracing all aspects of you, including the love you carry for the one you lost. Understand that you deserve a love that honors your past, embraces your present, and holds space for your future. Set healthy boundaries, communicate your needs, and allow yourself to be seen and cherished.

Remember that love is not a finite resource. Your heart can expand to encompass love for your lost beloved and a new partner. Embrace the truth that love is abundant, boundless, and capable of weaving its magic into the tapestry of your life once again.

Throughout this dance of love, be patient with yourself. Healing is not a linear process; each step forward demonstrates your resilience. Permit yourself to pause, reflect, and tend to any wounds that resurface. The path to love is as much about self-discovery as it is about connecting with another soul.

Trust your wisdom and intuition. Listen to your heart, for it knows the path to fulfillment and joy. As you navigate the complexities of seeking new love and intimacy after loss, know that I stand with you, holding space for your healing and celebrating the strength within you.

Honoring Sacred Memories While Embracing New Connections

As you open your heart to new connections, you must honor the memories of your loved one who has passed. This delicate balance between cherishing the past and embracing the present speaks to the depth of your love and the resilience of your spirit.

The memories you hold are sacred, intricately woven into your being, connecting you to your beloved and the experiences you shared. In honoring these memories, you acknowledge the profound impact your loved one had on your life and the enduring bond that transcends the physical realm.

Remember, honoring the past does not mean remaining trapped within it. On the contrary, your loved one would want nothing more than to see you continue to live a life of joy and fulfillment. They would like you to embrace the fullness of your being and be open to the blessings that await you.

Honoring your loved one's memories while opening yourself to new connections cultivates gratitude. Be grateful for the love you shared, the lessons learned, and the growth that has emerged from the experience of loss. Find comfort in knowing that your love for your beloved can coexist with the love you can give and receive from others.

Please do not shy away from vulnerability, for it is through vulnerability that authentic connections are forged. When you open your heart to another, share your joys and sorrows, and express your longing for love, you create a space for genuine connection to thrive. Trust that those meant to be in your life will honor and hold sacred the memory of your loved one.

In this journey of honoring the past while embracing the present, be gentle with yourself. There may be moments of guilt or feeling like you are betraying your beloved's memory. But know that love is expansive, and your capacity to love is boundless. Your loved one would want you to experience the fullness of love and companionship that life has to offer.

As you navigate this sacred path, remember that the love you share with your loved one is eternal. Their presence will forever be woven into the tapestry of your life. Embrace moments of joy, let laughter fill your days, and revel in the warmth of new connections. In doing so, you honor the memory of your beloved, for love is a legacy that transcends time and space.

Remember that your capacity to love and be loved is boundless. As you nurture self-compassion and self-worth, you create a solid foundation upon which new relationships can flourish. Trust in your resilience and ability to weave a tapestry of love that honors both the past and the present.

Chapter 8: I Hope You Dance: Opening Your Heart Again to Love

Lesson: Navigating Love and Relationships After Loss

This lesson will delve into the delicate process of navigating love and relationships after experiencing loss.

- **The Heart's Resilience**: Understand how the heart can heal and open up to new relationships while honoring the past.

Exercise: Exploring Self-Love and Self-Care

1. Find a serene and peaceful space to focus on self-reflection.
2. Begin by taking a few deep breaths to center yourself.
3. Write your thoughts and feelings about self-love and self-care in your journal. How have these concepts played a role in your healing journey so far?
4. List five ways you can practice self-love and self-care regularly. These could be simple activities like meditation, leisure time in nature, or a favorite hobby.
5. Choose one self-care activity from your list and commit to doing it regularly. This will be your self-love ritual.
6. Reflect on the importance of self-love and self-care in healing and opening your heart to love again.

Activity: Create a Love and Healing Vision Board

1. Gather magazines, images, quotes, and art supplies like scissors, glue, and a large poster board or canvas.

2. Set an intention for your vision board: "I am open to love and healing."

3. Begin flipping through magazines and selecting images, words, or phrases that resonate with your intention. These could relate to self-love, healing, and the love you wish to attract.

4. Arrange your chosen elements on the poster board or canvas in a visually appealing and meaningful way.

5. Use the glue to secure your chosen items in place.

6. Once your vision board is complete, take a moment to gaze at it and absorb the energy and intentions you have infused into it.

7. Place your vision board where you can see it regularly, such as your bedroom or a meditation space. Let it serve as a reminder of your openness to love and healing.

This lesson encourages you to explore the possibilities of love and relationships after experiencing loss. Practicing self-love and self-care by creating a love and healing vision board is a positive step towards opening your heart to new connections while honoring your past and the healing journey you have embarked upon.

Chapter Nine
From Sorrow to Serenity: Reconstructing Life After Loss

"The wound is the place where the Light enters you."
~ Rumi

Brenda's Story

Brenda carried the weight of guilt and sorrow for over three decades. The loss of her young son, Darryl, in a tragic accident haunted her daily. She could not help but blame herself for what happened, even though she knew deep down it was not her fault. The grief became a heavy shroud around her heart, which suffocated her with regret and sorrow.

One day, as she sat in her quiet living room filled with memories of Darryl, Brenda's friend, Lisa, told her about me and that I had helped many people find closure and peace after losing loved ones. Brenda was skeptical but also desperate to relieve the agony that gripped her for so long. She decided to give it a try.

Lisa accompanied Brenda to my office to help her feel more at ease, and once she was settled, we began the session.

The Mourning After

"Thank you for coming, Brenda," I said gently. "I sympathize with your pain and am here to help you connect with the young child on the other side."

With a deep breath, Brenda nodded, tears forming in her eyes. I closed my eyes to better tune in to the frequency of the realm of the departed.

I told Brenda, "I sense a young boy's energy, full of life and laughter. He's reaching out to you, almost as if asking to be picked up."

Brenda smiled and said, "Yes, even though Darryl was five years old, he always wanted me to pick him up and swing him around."

"I see him," I continued. "He's standing in a field wearing red shorts and a red shirt, and he's smiling, and I am sensing you have a picture of what I am describing. He pointed to a scar on his knee from falling off his bicycle and said the ice you put on it was so cold, it made him giggle. I can hear his laughter, and he wants you to know he's at peace now."

Tears streamed down Brenda's face as she pulled the described picture up on her phone to confirm that Darryl was right there with her, telling her he was all right.

"I need you to understand something, Brenda," I said with conviction and compassion. "Peter wants you to know that his passing was not your fault. It was an accident, and you could have done nothing to prevent it."

Brenda sobbed, feeling a profound mixture of relief and grief. She had carried the guilt for so long, and now, hearing these words from her son, it was as if a weight was finally lifting from her shoulders.

I continued to relay Darryl's messages, describing his vibrant spirit, the joy he experienced in the afterlife, and his love for his mother. He assured Brenda that he was watching over her, guiding her through life's challenges, and celebrating her triumphs.

Brenda felt a deep sense of healing and closure as the session continued. She knew that this encounter was the moment she had been waiting for, the opportunity to finally let go of the guilt that had tormented her for so long.

When the session concluded, Brenda left my office with a newfound peace. She realized that Darryl's love was eternal. He held no blame or resentment towards her, and he wanted nothing more than for her to find happiness and release the burden of guilt.

Over the following weeks and months, Brenda's life transformed. She gradually let go of the self-blame that had consumed her for over 30 years. She began to heal and find joy in life again, knowing that her beloved son was with her in spirit, supporting and loving her every step.

That single mediumship session, coupled with her faith and a new therapist, gave Brenda the closure she needed to move forward, honor Darryl's memory with love and gratitude, and live a life that would make her and her son proud.

Surrendering to the Depths of Sorrow

In the stillness of grief, where the world seems to stand still, and the weight of loss is an anchor around our hearts, we encounter sorrow in its purest form. It is a place where the pain feels bottomless, the tears flow like an endless river, and the ache in our souls seems unbearable. Yet, we find the seeds of transformation and growth within this crucible of sorrow.

Sorrow is not our enemy; it is a faithful companion on the journey of loss. It is the raw and unfiltered expression of love for the one we have lost, the testament to the depth of our connection. As we delve into the art of surrendering to sorrow, we must first acknowledge its presence without judgment. To surrender to sorrow is not an act of weakness; it is an act of profound courage and vulnerability. It means allowing ourselves to be messy and imperfect, experiencing whatever arises without judgment, and grieving uniquely on our timeline. Feeling the pain, weeping, rage, and grief is okay. This is not a sign of weakness but a testament to our capacity to love deeply.

When we fully allow ourselves to feel the pain in these moments of quiet reflection, we can connect with the essence of our loved ones and let healing begin. We honor the departed's memory by acknowledging their impact on our lives and the void their absence has created. In these moments, we can glimpse the beauty of the human experience, where love and loss are intertwined in a sacred dance. We must be gentle with ourselves and find the space for self-compassion, recognizing that grief is a heavy burden, not a linear process. There are no prescribed stages or timelines that we must adhere to. Each person's journey through sorrow is unique and shaped by their experiences, relationships, and coping mechanisms. It is okay to seek support from friends, family, or professionals to help navigate the turbulent waters of sorrow.

Surrendering to sorrow is not a one-time event but a process that unfolds over time. It is a journey that requires patience, self-compassion, and a willingness to embrace the full spectrum of human emotion, ultimately leading to healing and transformation. As we navigate unimaginable loss, we discover the resilience of the human spirit and the enduring power of love, finding peace and wisdom amid sorrow's embrace.

Honoring Your Emotions

Honoring your emotions is a crucial aspect of emotional well-being and self-awareness. Emotions are an inherent part of being human, and they serve as valuable signals that can guide our actions, decisions, and relationships. Rather than suppressing or dismissing our emotions, it is essential to acknowledge and honor them for several reasons.

First, honoring your emotions allows you to understand yourself better. Emotions are like messengers from your inner world, providing insights into your thoughts, values, and needs. When you take the time to recognize and validate your emotions, you gain a deeper understanding of what makes you tick. This self-awareness can lead to personal growth, enabling you to make more informed choices that align with your authentic self.

Second, honoring your emotions promotes mental and emotional well-being. Repressing or ignoring your feelings can lead to stress, anxiety, and even physical health issues. Acknowledging your feelings can release pent-up tension and reduce the burden on your mind and body. This emotional release process can be cathartic and help you achieve emotional balance and resilience.

Furthermore, honoring your emotions enhances your ability to connect with others. You become more empathetic and relatable when you acknowledge and express your feelings. Others can better understand your perspective, and you can relate to their emotions more effectively. This empathetic connection can strengthen your relationships, fostering trust and intimacy.

It is important to note that honoring your emotions does not mean giving in to every fleeting feeling or acting impulsively. Instead, it means recognizing your emotions without judgment, taking a moment to understand their source, and choosing how to respond in a way that aligns with your values and goals. In this way, you harness the power of your emotions as a source of wisdom and strength rather than allowing them to control or overwhelm you.

In conclusion, honoring your emotions is fundamental for personal growth, well-being, and healthy relationships. By acknowledging and understanding your feelings, you can navigate life's challenges with greater resilience and authenticity, ultimately leading to a more fulfilling and emotionally rich existence.

Allowing Your Tears to Flow

Allowing your tears to flow is an act of emotional authenticity and self-compassion. Tears are a natural and essential part of the human experience, and they serve several crucial functions in our emotional and physical well-being. Here are a few reasons why allowing yourself to cry can be a profoundly healing and liberating practice.

Tears are a means of emotional release. Shedding tears can be a powerful way to release pent-up emotions when overwhelmed by sadness, frustration, anger, or joy. Holding back tears can lead to emotional suppression, which may manifest as increased stress and tension. Allowing your tears to flow is like allowing yourself to release the emotional pressure valve, which can provide immediate relief and a sense of emotional lightness.

Crying is a form of self-compassion. It is acknowledging your pain, struggles, or vulnerabilities without judgment. In a world that often encourages us to be stoic or hide our emotions, allowing yourself to cry is an act of self-acceptance. It is a reminder that it is okay not to be okay and a step toward self-healing and self-compassion. When you embrace your tears, you tell yourself your feelings are valid and deserve acknowledgment.

Tears also have physiological benefits. They contain stress hormones and toxins, so when you cry, you expel harmful elements from your body. This cleansing process can leave you feeling physically and emotionally refreshed. It is like a natural detox for your mind and spirit.

Allowing your tears to flow can strengthen your emotional resilience. It is a way of processing and working through difficult emotions. When you cry, you are not escaping your feelings but confronting them head-on. This can help you gain clarity, find closure, and move forward with greater emotional strength and balance.

In essence, allowing your tears to flow is an act of self-compassion, a form of emotional release, and a step toward greater emotional resilience. It is a reminder that vulnerability is not a weakness but a sign of your humanity. By embracing your tears, you embrace yourself and the full spectrum of human emotions, ultimately leading to greater emotional well-being and authenticity. So, when the tears well up, do not hold back—let them flow, for they carry the potential for healing and growth.

Open Your Heart

Opening your heart and embracing vulnerability can be a challenging but rewarding journey toward deep emotional healing. It takes courage to let go of the shields and defenses we have built to protect ourselves, but it is through vulnerability that we can truly heal.

During times of grief, it is natural to want to shield ourselves from more pain. However, these barriers can prevent us from fully embracing the healing process. By consciously releasing them, we create space for authentic healing to occur.

Even though it may seem difficult to open our hearts during times of pain, it is within this vulnerability that we can experience profound transformation. By embracing our tenderness, we can connect with our hearts and the hearts of others.

It is important to remember that opening our hearts does not mean disregarding our pain or vulnerability. It means embracing them and allowing ourselves to be seen and supported in our journey. Surrounding ourselves with compassionate loved ones can create a nurturing environment supporting our healing and allowing our hearts to bloom.

As you embark on this courageous path of opening your heart, remember to trust in the resilience of your spirit and the transformative power it holds. May you find strength in surrendering to the tenderness of an open heart on this journey.

Seeking Support and Connection

During times of healing, it is so important to feel the support and connection of others. Explore how reaching out to loved ones, support groups, or professional counselors can help you find comfort and strength and discover how vulnerability can lead to transformation and growth.

Your loved ones can be a significant source of comfort when you are grieving. They can offer empathy and understanding by sharing your emotions and experiences with them. Their support can remind you that you are not alone and that your feelings are valid.

Support groups, whether in person or online, can offer a sense of solace and understanding through shared experiences. Connecting with others who have gone through similar struggles allows you to find compassion and a safe place to express yourself. This can help you receive support from people who understand the depth of your pain.

Professional counselors and therapists can offer specialized support and guidance as you navigate your healing journey. Their safe and confidential space allows you to process your emotions and grief and receive guidance toward healing. Seeking professional help shows strength and self-compassion, acknowledging that you deserve dedicated care during this challenging time.

It takes courage and strength to seek support. But by allowing yourself to be vulnerable and accepting help during your most difficult moments, you create opportunities for deep healing and connection. Remember, you are not alone on your journey. Contact your loved ones, join a support group, or seek professional guidance. By embracing the power of shared experiences and compassion, you can find comfort, strength, and resilience on your path to healing.

Practice Self-Care

During times of sorrow, it is crucial to prioritize your well-being with self-care practices that nourish and support your mind, body, and spirit. Remember, taking care of yourself is not selfish; it is an act of self-love and preservation. Identify the practices that bring you peace and comfort. It could be something as simple as taking a warm bath, walking in nature, meditating, or spending time with loved ones who uplift your spirit. These practices can provide a sense of inner nourishment. Make self-care a priority daily, allowing yourself the space and time to tend to your well-being.

Create self-compassionate rituals that honor your grief journey and facilitate healing. Allow yourself to acknowledge and celebrate your emotions through intentional ceremonies, such as lighting a candle, journaling, or creating a sacred space to reflect and connect with your inner self. These rituals become acts of self-compassion, providing a safe container for your grief and helping you navigate the healing process.

Remember that practicing self-care is a sacred act of compassion and self-preservation. Give yourself the grace to prioritize your well-being during this difficult time. Cultivate activities that nurture your mind, body, and spirit. May you find relief and strength as you embrace the transformative power of self-nurturing.

Find Meaning in Sorrow

Reflecting on the potential for transformation and growth within sorrow takes courage. It is not an easy journey, but examining our experiences and uncovering the more profound lessons they offer can lead us to newfound strength, empathy, and appreciation for life.

Searching for meaning and lessons can bring comfort and guidance on your healing journey when you are deep in grief. Explore the values and qualities that have emerged or been tested through your sorrow and consider ways to honor your loved one's memory or support others grieving. By seeking meaning, you can create a narrative that honors your journey and brings purpose to your healing process.

Remember that even the darkest experiences can lead to wisdom and growth. Like a seed that must be buried in darkness to sprout and reach for the light, sorrow can become a catalyst for transformation and strength. Trust in your innate wisdom, knowing it can guide you through the darkest times and lead you toward a deeper understanding of yourself and life.

Redefine Identity and Purpose

It can be challenging to navigate the grief process and understand how it affects us. Loss can change so much about our lives, including how we see ourselves and our roles in the world. It is important to take the time to reflect on these changes and how they have impacted our identities.

Let yourself grieve the parts of your identity that have been lost or transformed. It is okay to mourn the person you used to be and the life you used to have. But also know that this loss can create space for a new sense of self to emerge.

Creating a new narrative for yourself can be a powerful way to honor your journey and move forward. This new story can incorporate the wisdom and resilience you have gained through your experiences of sorrow. Consider what values, passions, and desires hold meaning for you now. You can let go of societal expectations and embrace an authentic path.

Your inner wisdom and intuition can guide you towards a sense of purpose that honors your unique journey. Use the lessons and insights you gained from your loss experience to inform your purpose moving forward. Trust that the potential for profound growth and a renewed sense of purpose lies within your sorrow.

Remember, this is a personal and transformative process. Take it one step at a time, and be gentle with yourself. May you find solace and strength in unfolding your identity, and may your rediscovered purpose bring meaning and fulfillment as you navigate the path of grief to peace.

As you continue on the healing path, let love be your guide. It is a powerful force that can provide comfort, strength, and healing amidst the pain of grief. Be kind to yourself and practice self-love and self-compassion. Treat yourself with the same care and understanding you would give a dear friend. Remember the love you hold for those you have lost, and let it be a beacon of light, reminding you of the deep connection that transcends physical presence.

Through self-care, finding meaning, and embracing love and joy, we infuse our healing journey with light and find strength in new connections. This chapter serves as a guide and reminder that healing is possible, and from the depths of sorrow, we can emerge into a place of serenity and peace. Trust in your resilience and embrace the transformative power of the journey from sorrow to serenity.

Chapter 9: From Sorrow to Serenity: Reconstructing Life After Loss

Lesson: Rebuilding Your Life After Loss

In this lesson, we will explore rebuilding your life after the profound experience of loss.

- **A Path to Serenity**: Discover strategies and insights for navigating the journey from sorrow to serenity.

Exercise: Setting Goals for Your Healing Journey

1. Find a peaceful, quiet space to focus on your healing journey.
2. Take a few deep breaths to center yourself and bring your attention to the present moment.
3. Write down your short-term and long-term goals for your healing journey in your journal. Consider what you hope to achieve regarding emotional well-being, personal growth, and spiritual development.
4. Break down each goal into smaller, actionable steps. These steps should be specific, measurable, achievable, relevant, and time-bound (SMART goals).
5. Create a timeline for when you intend to achieve each step. Be realistic and compassionate with yourself.
6. Reflect on how accomplishing these goals will improve your healing and well-being.

Activity: Create a "Life Reimagined" Collage

1. Gather magazines, images, quotes, and art supplies like scissors, glue, and a large poster board or canvas.

2. Set the intention for your collage: "I am reconstructing my life with purpose and serenity."

3. Begin flipping through magazines and selecting images, words, or phrases that resonate with your intention. Look for visuals representing your goals, dreams, and the life you want to create.

4. Arrange your chosen elements on the poster board or canvas, visually representing your reimagined life. Allow your creativity to flow freely.

5. Use the glue to secure your chosen items in place.

6. Once your "Life Reimagined" collage is complete, take a moment to gaze at it and absorb the energy and intentions you have infused into it.

7. Place your collage in a prominent location where you can see it daily. Let it inspire and remind you of the path you are forging toward serenity and reconstruction.

This lesson empowers you to set goals for your healing journey and visualize the life you want to create. By breaking down your goals into manageable steps and creating a "Life Reimagined" collage, you are actively participating in rebuilding your life after loss, infusing it with purpose and serenity.

Chapter Ten
In Their Own Words:
Stories of Healing and Resilience

"Grief and resilience live together."
~ **Michelle Obama**

Grief can feel like an insurmountable mountain in the aftermath of loss, casting a shadow over our lives and leaving us yearning for solace. Yet, even in the darkest moments, the human spirit has an incredible capacity for healing and resilience. In this chapter of "The Mourning After," I invite you to hear the heartfelt stories of those who have embarked on their unique journeys of grief and found a path toward light and hope.

The client testimonials shared within these pages testify to the power of human connection, the strength of the human spirit, and the transformative nature of embracing our grief. Each story serves as a reminder that while grief is an individual experience, it is also a shared human condition. Through these narratives, we gain insights into how grief manifests itself and the varied paths to healing.

In the words of our clients, you will witness the raw emotions of loss and the depths of despair gripping their hearts. Yet, amidst their pain, you will also discover the seeds of resilience and the flickers of hope that emerge. These testimonials offer glimpses into the moments of clarity and understanding that changed their perspectives and helped them navigate the intricate labyrinth of grief.

Within these pages, you will encounter individuals from all walks of life—each with a unique story. Their experiences will remind you that grief knows no boundaries of age, race, or background. It touches us all, leaving an indelible mark on our lives. However, it is how we choose to respond to grief that shapes our journey.

As you read the heartfelt accounts, you will witness the power of support and compassion—both given and received, highlighting the profound impact that therapy, church, community, and embracing mediumship can have on the healing process. In addition, they serve as a reminder that no one should navigate the tumultuous waters of grief alone.

The stories shared in this chapter speak of resilience. They testify to the human capacity to rebuild, find meaning amid chaos, and emerge from the depths of grief with renewed purpose. They remind us that while grief may forever change us, it does not define us. It is a chapter in our lives but does not have to be the final chapter.

So, as you immerse yourself in the client testimonials of "The Mourning After," may these stories serve as beacons of hope and inspiration. May they remind you that healing is possible, that your pain is valid, and that you are not alone in your journey. Together, let us honor the resilience and strength of those who have bravely shared their stories as we continue our quest for healing and embrace the dawn of a new chapter.

Efia

My personal and professional life thrived through the worst of the pandemic, but they both took a turn in the summer of 2021. My mother's dementia had progressed, and I moved back into our family home to help care for her. Unfortunately, this set off an *avalanche*. My 6-year 'situationship' ended, and my once dream job had become unbearable. I crammed my life into my old bedroom since my sister, her husband, and her son were there, too. Clutter and lack of privacy were suffocating me. I was lonely, angry, overeating, already grieving my mother, and headed for a deep depression. I thought I had found a therapist, but her *direct* approach insisted I move back out. I thought I was going to lose my mind.

Then, while scrolling on social media one night, I found a dear friend and fellow therapist's post about Dr. Lakara Foster and was IMMEDIATELY intrigued. However, when I learned she was a Black woman, I was SOLD and booked an in-person session that October.

It was fascinating how quickly and easily she tapped in, sensing one of my grandmothers tell her to "get to it"! My father transitioned 15 years ago; my oldest brother was three years before that. Yet, BOTH came through. It was not just a feel-good reading- they shared messages with Dr. Foster for me to set boundaries, deepen my spirituality, and stop trying to do too much! My dad's spirit even showed off a little, giving her the name of an old family friend—the same one my mom had gotten a card from the mail the week before! He had been there with us, looking at the picture over her shoulder.

I attended her Virtual Vision Board Party in January 2023, which was ANOTHER fantastic experience. So far, my vision has manifested, and I have quit the job and found love again!

Fast-forward to November 2022. I took my sister to Dr. Foster's live group reading in Atlanta. Don't you know the FIRST person to come through was my father AGAIN, out of all the ancestors in the room? Just as he was in life as a pastor and counselor, he was often the first to speak, pray, and offer encouragement. This time, he had a message about watching over my living, estranged brother, which would offer consolation to our worried mother.

Dr. Foster's gifts are undeniable, but the unexpected takeaway was that her medium readings helped me process and heal my grief. I had hoped, but now I *know* my dad and other ancestors are always with me.

My experiences with Dr. Foster enhanced my therapy practice because I encourage medium readings for my clients experiencing grief and loss. To anyone who fears this energy exchange, please know it is life-changing. Yes, therapy has its benefits, but there are places within us that words and other conventional methods cannot touch.

Efia Miles, Lithonia, GA

Natasha

The unexpected passing of my husband left me with inconsolable grief and a longing for answers that no one could provide. I missed my husband dearly, but I understood the fragility of life and that all things must end. So much of my grief was centered around the uncertainty of what happens after we pass and the thought of my husband being unable to experience our children, for he loved being a father.

For months, I researched death, various religions, and the afterlife or lack thereof. Psychic medium experiences frequently appeared on my social media timelines, so I researched them extensively. My search led me to Dr. Lakara Foster. After discovering her, I waited several months before scheduling an appointment. When I finally booked it, I created a fake email address and only used my first name since I was still skeptical. My expectations were not high, so if she could not provide me with undeniable proof that she was communicating with my husband, I would accept that we would cease to exist after death. However, if she could provide evidence, I would feel lighter knowing he still lives eternally.

Being the skeptic that I am, at the beginning of my session, I was not completely sold on the realness of her gift. However, she mentioned detailed situations that, even if she had all my information and researched me, she could not have found it online. One detail she shared with me was my undeniable proof, and I was sure then that my husband was there with us. He communicated to Dr. Foster to mention his black hat. She asked me the significance of the black hat he was bringing up. I explained that when he passed, he was wearing a black beanie that had fallen off his head when he collapsed from the carbon monoxide poisoning. The day after his passing, I returned to where the accident happened to grab his black hat. It has been on my car headrest ever since. It was my undeniable proof because he was always my passenger driver, and I intentionally put it in my car as a reminder that he was still present with me. I have never shared that information with not even my closest people, and for her to bring it up was mind-blowing.

Leaving my session, I felt a closeness to my husband, not in my ideal way, but an intimacy that I have not been able to feel since his passing. I left there telling him our dynamic is a little different, but he is still my husband, so he better not connect with any other energies up there. I laugh now because it sounds wild, but we both know I am serious. My grief has shifted since my session; the proof that he still gets to experience us and continues to exist lightens my heart. Dr. Foster's gift has inspired me to dive more into my spirituality and explore psychic mediumship abilities that might be buried in me. It has brought me so much peace, and I recommend it to anyone grieving. You have nothing to lose but so much to gain.

Natasha Quiles

Penny

I grew up in a broken family. When I was six, my parents relocated from their hometown of Hammond, LA, losing most relationships with my extended family. I never had the opportunity to know my grandparents on my mother's side of the family. On my father's side, my memories of them only go up until age six, when we moved away. The absence of my grandparents has always been a source of sadness and shame for me. I have never experienced the joy of having large family gatherings or participating in cherished family traditions passed down over generations for special holidays.

As my understanding of African Spirituality has grown, I have developed a strong desire to connect with and learn about my ancestors. Despite growing up in a strict Christian household where discussions of ancestors and related topics were deemed "witchcraft," I now recognize that our ancestors continue to exist in spirit after passing from this life. As I deconstruct the theology taught as a child, I am eager to explore this critical aspect of my heritage.

I recently came across Dr. Foster's unique gift of mediumship while listening to Dr. Carlton Pearson's podcast. Her radiance caught my attention, and I booked a session with her. During the reading, Dr. Foster conveyed messages from my beloved paternal grandmother, a woman of great faith. It was touching when Dr. Foster brought up my butterfly tattoos, which were not visible to her in our session, and I knew this message was being communicated from beyond. This made me emotional as I felt my grandmother's presence and realized she loved me dearly. Being someone who grew up feeling disconnected, this experience was heartwarming and much needed. As a result, I now see butterflies as a sacred symbol of my grandmother being with me.

During our session, Dr. Foster reassured me that my difficult and estranged relationship with my father was not my fault. She shared a profound moment when my grandmother said, "He thinks he's right, but he's not. It is not you. He is not well," without mentioning my father or our relationship. This statement lifted the weight of guilt that I had been carrying for so long. I had always questioned if there was something I could have done differently to mend our relationship or if I was the cause of our brokenness. Hearing my grandmother's words, especially about her son, gave me a sense of freedom. I hold onto this memory dearly, knowing I am not alone brings comfort. I am grateful to God and Dr. Foster for this incredible gift that has helped me heal.

Penny Green

Chandra

Having spiritual gifts is a true blessing. I have always felt that there might be undiscovered gifts within me. That is why when I saw Dr. Lakara Foster on TV, I felt an instant connection with her. I immediately researched ways to meet her. It could be because of the subject matter she was discussing or perhaps because she embodies Black girl magic. Nonetheless, she has been an absolute blessing to me.

A few years ago, my life took a heartbreaking turn when my precious son, Cameron James, was born stillborn. The experience was emotionally devastating and brought me to the brink of death during the emergency C-section. In addition, the trauma left me grappling with immense guilt and countless questions.

When I first met Lakara, I poured out my heart, expressing my deep longing to connect with my beloved son, Cameron. However, her response caught me off guard. She paused, contemplating my words, and then uttered something that sent shivers down my spine, "You want to connect with one baby... I see TWO."

Those words struck me like lightning because, in my mind, I had only experienced three pregnancies. My firstborn son, now an 11-year-old, my angel son, Cameron, and my cherished rainbow baby daughter, who is now five years old. Confusion clouded my thoughts until, after careful reflection, I realized the truth behind her words—the identity of the second spirit she spoke of. About a year after I lost Cameron, I became pregnant with my daughter. Throughout the pregnancy, medical professionals shared that I had an extra sack in my wound for a fetus that never developed. After researching, I discovered that this phenomenon is called a "vanishing twin." So, after losing Cameron, our focus was majorly on the filled sack and the new life forming in my belly.

I was utterly astonished by Dr. Foster's profound insights, which validated her authenticity and left me in awe of her abilities. The revelation about the vanishing twin was a profoundly personal secret, known to only a select few of my loved ones. Astonishingly, I had not even disclosed this information to my mother. Yet, during that transformative first meeting with Dr. Foster, she delved into the depths of spirit and conveyed messages to me about the events that transpired on that fateful day, unraveling the purpose behind that poignant experience.

In the weeks following our conversation, I repeatedly reflected on the words she had shared with me. Like puzzle pieces gradually falling into place, the significance of her messages began to crystallize in my mind. With each passing moment of reflection, her words resonated even deeper, illuminating a profound truth I had previously overlooked.

Since that initial call, my ongoing conversations with Dr. Foster have been remarkable. Her spiritual guidance and unwavering intuition have proven accurate and invaluable. I cannot express enough gratitude for the closure she has provided me with, as the burden of guilt surrounding my son's untimely passing has significantly diminished under her compassionate guidance.

Not only has Dr. Foster brought solace to my own heart, but she has also extended her helping hand to numerous friends and family members who sought her support. She has become the beacon of closure that enables us all to move forward, offering the profound wisdom and insight that can only come from a place of divine connection. Her presence serves as the still, small voice of the spirit, gently nudging us toward healing, understanding, and the peace we earnestly seek.

Mrs. Chandra McKinney-Clarke, M.S.

Dr. Tina

At a time when the weight of burdens pressed heavily upon my shoulders, I sought solace through a reading with Dr. Foster. Among the sorrows I carried, one of the deepest wounds was the unsolved murder of my beloved son. The weight of guilt silently consumed me, unshared with anyone around me.

In the haunting depths of my soul, I still vividly remember the last time I saw my son donning a bulletproof vest in the streets of Miami. Deep within my spirit, I carried an unspoken knowing, a profound intuition that whispered his time in this realm was numbered. Helplessly, I watched in silent anguish, aware of the risks he faced, yearning to protect him from the dangerous path he had chosen. Yet, I felt powerless, a witness to his descent into a life from which he could not easily escape.

Then, as if the world shattered, my worst nightmare became a devastating reality—a call informing me of his tragic fate. In that heart-wrenching moment, my world crumbled, and my heart shattered into a thousand pieces. The anguish I felt seemed incomprehensible and unnatural to bury my son. And in that same breath, an overwhelming sense of self-blame consumed me. I questioned whether I had failed him or could have done something more to steer him towards a different path, even though deep down, I knew the complexities of his choices extended far beyond my reach.

As the years unfolded, grief became an unwavering companion, and with its presence came the haunting thoughts of what could have been—what my son could have become had he been granted more time, for his talent was undeniable. The weight of countless "what-ifs" and unanswerable "whys" burdened my heart. Yet, amidst the shadows of sorrow, a curious occurrence began to unfold in my life.

I started noticing the presence of a vibrant red bird, appearing unexpectedly in the most unlikely of places as I traversed through life's journey. Its persistent presence struck me as peculiar, yet an indescribable joy would fill me whenever it came into view. This bird had become my silent companion, accompanying me wherever I traveled.

Whether perched on a tree branch outside my window, resting gracefully on a fence in my backyard, or even delicately perching on a windowsill across the vast expanse of the United States, the red bird manifested itself in countless forms, capturing my attention repeatedly. Its mysterious appearance held a profound significance, stirring emotions within me that words failed to convey.

The significance of the enigmatic red bird that had graced my life with its presence became abundantly clear during my reading with Dr. Foster. A revelation unfolded in moments that would forever transform my perspective. As I shared my story, she posed a question that caught me off guard, leaving me gasping for air. And then, in a stunning realization, the message from my son began to unfold.

With unwavering certainty, my son spoke through Dr. Foster, instructing her to inquire about the red bird. How could she have known about this profound connection I had experienced? In that sacred moment, I knew beyond doubt that my son's spirit was indeed present, orchestrating this extraordinary encounter. Through Dr. Foster's words, my son conveyed a message that resonated deep within my soul.

With love and compassion, he assured me that his passing was not my fault. There was nothing I could have done to alter the course of events. Instead, in his infinite wisdom, he acknowledged my role as his best mother, affirming that he would choose me repeatedly if given a chance. He urged me to release the burden of guilt, forgive myself, and embrace a path of healing and peace. And, with overwhelming clarity, he revealed that he had become the red bird—a celestial messenger, reminding me of his eternal presence.

In that moment of revelation, an indescribable sense of tranquility washed over me, intermingled with tears of release and joy. From that day forward, whenever the red bird graced my sight, I knew it was an invitation to converse with my beloved son. In those sacred moments, an ineffable connection was forged, evoking a radiant smile upon my face and infusing my heart with an everlasting sense of joy.

Words cannot adequately express my gratitude to Dr. Foster for delivering this profound message to my son. Her extraordinary gift has guided me from pain, grief, and confusion toward a transformative journey of joy, peace, and forgiveness. The impact of her intervention in my life is immeasurable, and I will forever cherish the blessings she has bestowed upon me. My heart overflows with gratitude for the profound healing and solace she has facilitated, forever altering the trajectory of my emotional and spiritual well-being. Thank you, Dr. Foster, from the depths of my soul, for the gift of clarity, restoration, and eternal gratitude.

Kathryn

The most devastating loss in my life occurred on May 1st, 2001, when I had to witness my beloved mother's transition. Standing by her bedside, the weight of helplessness engulfed me, and I struggled to process the magnitude of the moment. Then, as she took her final breath, she whispered those tender words, "I love you," before peacefully closing her eyes for the last time. It left me pondering a profound question: Where does love go after a transition?

Amid my unbearable sorrow, I found myself in the presence of Dr. Foster. Lost, fearful, and profoundly alone, I carried an unrelenting sadness that had no end. My experience felt isolated, devoid of any comparison. I questioned my motives, wondering if I was selfish to yearn for my mother's presence again. Family and friends, struggling to comprehend my grief, often offered dismissive remarks, telling me to "get over it" or reminding me that she was no longer here. I was left without a guidebook or blueprint to navigate the intricacies of such a profound loss. Instead, I clung to the belief I had been taught that once we depart this earthly realm, nothing else exists beyond.

Having witnessed television shows exploring the realms of crossing over and the role of psychic mediums, I could never have fathomed that I would one day find myself engaging with a medium and experiencing a profound connection with my mother. It seemed like an unimaginable possibility within the confines of my world. However, fate had its plans, and twenty years later, during an airing of VH1 Couples Retreat, Dr. Foster was introduced as a psychic medium. This serendipitous encounter sparked my curiosity, prompting me to reach out and embark on a journey I had never anticipated.

The medium reading that ensued was nothing short of intriguing. Excitement tinged with uncertainty coursed through me as I wondered what this extraordinary experience would unveil. It was an evening I will forever cherish, May 13, 2021, when our first session occurred. Yet, nervousness gripped me, and I found myself questioning the authenticity of it all. "Is this real?" I asked myself, half-expecting dramatic lights flickering or tables levitating. Yet, the reality was far more organic and serene than what popular media had portrayed.

Under Dr. Foster's gentle introduction and expert guidance, the stage was set for our profound session. I expressed my desire to connect with a specific individual, and she gracefully initiated the process. In awe, I closely observed as she attentively listened and meticulously captured her impressions through sketches on paper. Her interactions felt like an ethereal, unspoken conversation laden with profound significance. Each image she drew unfolded deliberately, carrying a deep personal meaning that resonated with me instantaneously. Through these drawings, a hidden tapestry of connection and understanding was unveiled, touching the depths of my soul.

Dr. Foster's wisdom extended beyond the session itself. She generously shared her expertise in fostering a connection with my dear mother. She guided me through the realms of intuition and meditation, shedding light on their transformative power. No question was off-limits as we navigated this mystical journey together. Reflecting upon those initial moments, I now realize I was at a loss for what to ask, think, or feel. Yet, with Dr. Foster's patient guidance and unwavering reassurance, I opened myself to her remarkable gift with heartfelt gratitude.

My journey alongside Dr. Foster continues to unfold, guiding me on a path of profound transformation and understanding. Through our shared exploration, I have delved into energy, forgiveness, and the intricate intersection between healing and personal growth. It is clear to me now that our meeting was not a coincidence but a purposeful alignment orchestrated by a higher power. Dr. Foster has graciously equipped me with invaluable tools, strategies, and resources that have empowered me to recognize and nurture my intuition.

Since that enlightening reading, my perspective on grief, clarity, and closure has shifted profoundly. It has become a catalyst for healing and transformation, unlocking a newfound capacity to embrace growth and love and restoring my faith. The reading served as a pivotal moment on my journey, illuminating pathways to healing and redefining my understanding of life's profound transitions.

Yet, this healing journey does not end here. Dr. Foster's guidance has challenged my preconceived notions of grief, after-death communication, and the special connection between mediumship and the eternal nature of love. Her wisdom has brought clarity and shown me that love transcends the boundaries of time and space. Despite the passage of two decades, I now wholeheartedly believe in the eternal presence of my mother's love. I am deeply grateful to Dr. Foster for this revelation, whose guidance and support have been instrumental in my healing journey.

Kathryn W.

Pariese

Meeting with a spiritual medium was never something I had considered until my uncle passed away suddenly. It devastated my family, leaving us grappling with so much tragedy. However, shortly before my uncle passed, I encountered Dr. Lakara. I watched a Facebook Live where she spoke about her gift as a medium and her ability to connect with those who have transitioned to the spiritual realm. When my uncle passed, I knew that meeting with her would bring me solace during such a challenging time. Meeting Dr. Lakara brought me so much peace, knowing that my uncle was at peace and still wearing his signature smile. I am forever grateful that I met her when I did and at the time when I needed her gift the most.

I am incredibly grateful for my encounter with Dr. Lakara, as it has completely transformed my perception of death. Through her guidance, I have learned that paying attention to signs allows me to receive messages from my uncle, even in his transition to the afterlife. This newfound understanding brings me immense comfort and happiness, knowing that my uncle's essence continues to exist eternally. Lakara has taught me a valuable lesson I will always carry.

Pariese Lewis

Erin

When I first sat down with Dr. Lakara Foster, we were having a friendly conversation on her couch, and she mentioned someone named Deanna. At the time, I did not think much of it. However, a few months later, I decided to book my first reading with Dr. Foster, which took place on August 16th. I will explain why that date is significant in just a moment.

Throughout our reading, we explored several topics instrumental in my spiritual journey. However, when my mother communicated, I finally received my sought-after closure. During the session, Dr. Foster asked me if the date, 8/16, was significant, but I could not recall anything. Then she mentioned seeing a cardinal and asked if red meant anything to me. I immediately thought of my maternal grandfather, whom I affectionately called Grandpa Red. That is when my mother began communicating with Dr. Foster. She revealed that our tumultuous relationship was due to her issues with my grandfather, but she assured me she was my ally and wanted me to continue speaking up. She also expressed her pride in me, which was incredibly meaningful.

After a satisfying reading, Dr. Foster and I enjoyed dinner on the patio. However, bees landed on me and my food, while no one else was affected. Later, I learned that this was a bee totem, signaling a fresh start for me and affirming the insights from my reading. As if to further confirm this, I saw on Facebook that my cousin Deanna had wished our late Grandpa Red a happy birthday on August 16th. When I called her to share my reading experience, she confirmed many of the details discussed and more.

I recently had a reading with Dr. Lakara Foster, who has an exceptional ability to follow her intuition and move when Spirit guides her. I must say, her reading was a life-changing experience for me. It helped me overcome long-held hurt, pain, and resentment and filled my heart with understanding, love, and appreciation. Dr. Foster was incredibly patient and thorough in her approach, and I eagerly look forward to my next reading with her.

Erin Sample

Wayne

I must admit that I entered my reading with Dr. Foster apprehensive. While in prayer, God spoke to me and said I needed to set up a session. There were several things consistently on my mind for years. I researched her unique gift and realized it was not much different from African tribes that spoke to ancestors via the priest or priestess. It also connected with Native American cultures that consistently communicate with ancestral spirits. As both are part of my history, I made the appointment.

I was at ease within the first five minutes. Dr. Foster did not know that I struggled with the death of my dad for the past 23 years. I was performing in a concert, so I was not there when he passed. Being absent at that moment kept me stuck with feelings of guilt for not being there, anger at him for leaving, and anger at my mom for not telling me he was sick. I learned to suppress these feelings by living each day, hoping he would be proud of me. The first words out of Dr. Foster's mouth were, "Your dad has been with me for days, and before I get into this reading, he wants me to let you know that he is proud of you. I only shared that information with a few people in my life; she had no connection to any of those individuals.

With all the loss and grief that plagued my life over the past few years, I was unsure what to expect. Several members of my family spoke to me during that session. It was a life-changing moment because I received so many confirmations.

When the session ended, I was uplifted and felt a sense of freedom I had not experienced in over two decades. Since that reading, I have lived my life with renewed purpose.

Dr. R. Wayne Woodson

Chapter 10: In Their Own Words: Stories of Healing and Resilience

Lesson: Learning from Stories of Healing

In this final chapter, we will explore the power of storytelling in the healing process and how sharing our journeys can inspire and support one another.

- **The Healing Tapestry of Stories**: Understand the significance of stories in our healing journeys.

Exercise: Share Your Healing Journey with Others

1. Find a safe and supportive space where you can share your healing journey. This could be with friends, family, a support group, or a therapist.

2. Prepare to share your story honestly and authentically. You can use your journal to jot down key points or emotions you want to convey.

3. Share your journey, focusing on the challenges you have faced, the lessons you have learned, and the transformations you have experienced.

4. Be open to listening to others' stories as well. Remember that healing is a collective experience, and you can draw inspiration and insights from others.

5. Reflect on how sharing your story and listening to others' stories impacts your healing process. Consider any new perspectives or connections you have gained.

Activity: Create a Community Healing Circle

1. Invite a group of individuals who have experienced loss and are on their healing journeys to participate in a community healing circle. This can be done in person or virtually.

2. Begin the circle with a moment of reflection or a short meditation to center everyone.

3. Encourage each participant to take turns sharing their healing journey, challenges, and moments of resilience.

4. Create an atmosphere of empathy, support, and non-judgment where everyone feels comfortable sharing.

5. As each person shares, others can listen actively and offer encouragement or understanding.

6. After everyone has had the opportunity to share, conclude the circle with a collective intention for continued healing and resilience.

7. Make the community healing circle a regular gathering to foster ongoing support and connection.

This chapter emphasizes the importance of storytelling in the healing process and the strength we find in sharing our journeys with others. By sharing your healing journey and participating in a community healing circle, you contribute to a collective tapestry of resilience and inspire those around you on their paths of healing and renewal.

Acknowledgments

God, I thank you! Even as I write these words, I feel the energy of Spirit, The Great Ancestors, Universal Consciousness, Oneness, or whatever you call the never-ending and constantly flowing energy. I know this book is "it," "the thing," "the purpose" for which I was created. I am here now, and I am ready. Thank you for allowing me to be a vessel, for the gift of mediumship, and for allowing me to help those who are grieving so that they may continue to do the will of the God of their understanding.

I stand on the precipice of this book, gazing back through the corridors of time, and my heart swells with gratitude for the many hands that have shaped me into the person I am today. Thank you to my past self for the unwavering determination and curiosity that set me on this path. You were the seed from which this journey grew.

To my present self, the one who weathered countless storms and found the strength to put pen to paper, I owe you my most profound appreciation. Your resilience and commitment brought these words to life.

And to my future self, who will continue to evolve and learn long after these pages have turned, I offer my hopes and aspirations. May you build upon the foundation we've laid here, and may your wisdom continue to grow.

To all the remarkable individuals who have graced my life, whether for a moment or a lifetime, you have poured love, support, and guidance into each version of me. Family, friends, mentors, and even strangers who offered a kind word, you have all played a part in this story.

I am eternally grateful to my parents, Ernest Sr., and Maggie Foster, who instilled in me a love for learning and a belief in endless possibilities. Your unwavering support has been my anchor.

Thank you to my brothers Ernest Jr. and Benjamin Sr. and your children Benjamin "Bj," Ernest III, "Baby Boo," Khloe, and Chance for your love and laughter through the years.

Dred Carpenter, You and Axel are "minez with a z." You constantly push me to be the best version of myself, and you have loved me relentlessly from the moment we "re-met."

To my friends, Jeff, Annette, Cornesha, Curtis, Red Summer, Courtney, Mia, Look Alive, Rolo, April, Rae, Requaya, August, Cheffy, and Hakim, who have stood by me through thick and thin, your laughter and camaraderie have been a balm for my soul.

To my mentors, Bishop O.C. Allen, Dr. Daniel Black, and Bishop Carlton Pearson, whose wisdom has illuminated my path, you have shaped my intellect and character in ways I can never fully repay.

To my Vision Church of Atlanta and UPPC Family, thank you for having my back and holding space for me to show up just as God created me. It has been a joy to serve with all of you.

To those who challenged me, doubted me, and pushed me beyond my comfort zone, you, too, have been instrumental. You forced me to grow, adapt, and become stronger.

To the countless authors, thinkers, and creators whose works have inspired and educated me, your words have been my companions on this journey.

I offer my deepest thanks to my readers, who have chosen to spend their precious time within these pages. You are the reason for this endeavor, and your engagement with my words is a gift beyond measure.

In closing, this book is a culmination of the past, a reflection of the present, and a tribute to the future. It is a testament to the power of community, the idea that we are all interconnected and that our individual stories are woven into the fabric of humanity. Thank you, from the bottom of my heart, for being a part of my story.

With boundless gratitude,

Dr. Lakara Foster

www.ingramcontent.com/pod-product-compliance
Lightning Source LLC
Chambersburg PA
CBHW072051290426
44110CB00014B/1639